E

“There is an o[illegible] cover. When it comes to Pastor CR Cali as author and the content of his new book, the Doctrine of Balaam, this is sage advice indeed. The outside man of Pastor Cali reveals an extreme form of paganism before his conversion, while his inner man unveils a beautiful soul that has been redeemed by Christ. The Doctrine of Balaam is essential to any thoughtful Christian who is done with regulating the murder of babies by abortion but will labor God’s way to completely end it. In order to outlaw abortion altogether, Pastor Cali has held up the language, strategies, and failed public policies of the secular Pro-life movement to the light of Scripture. It is there only that we discover the revealed character of God contained in His commandments, and His criteria Biblically to establish justice on the behalf of our preborn neighbor. What we will find in that much needed comparison is the secular Pro-life movement that has influenced much of the church has been weighed in the balance and found wanting. Using two primary premises, the serpent’s doubtful lie, “Hath God said,” and the righteous and just assertion of “Thus saith the Lord,” Pastor Cali separates the wheat from the chaff. He exposes the sin of God’s people as we have shown partiality when it comes to God’s demand for justice for the preborn. I highly recommend this book. I would encourage all to study its contents. If, perhaps, you find yourself a part of the secular Pro-life movement that has inadvertently prolonged the suffering and injustice against the preborn, simply repent and acknowledge the truth that has the power to set free. Then, by God’s grace, commit to fight this battle for the liberation of the preborn according to God’s will, word, and way.”

—Rev. Rusty Lee Thomas National Director, *Operation Save America.*

"The pro-life movement has failed to end abortion in America because it was built upon humanistic, utilitarian presupposition and pragmatism. A standard built upon Christian presupposition and the law and Word of God is needed to outlaw this bloodshed and establish justice for the preborn. Cali has provided such a standard here. Written with sound reason and the heart of a pastor, this work will help many see that God's Word truly does speak to all matters of life, and will lay a foundation in the lives of men to see the spilt innocent blood of our preborn neighbors ended in our nation."
—Matt Trewhella, Pastor of Mercy Seat Christian Church, Director Missionaries to the Preborn

"If you have ever wondered why the pro-life movement contradicts itself and the Word of God (with enormous evangelical support), this book is for you. Cali has given the true Church a valuable weapon in her arsenal. Well researched both historically and Biblically, Cali proves that the secular pro-life industry is both self-defeating and compromised. Jesus Christ and His gospel is highly exalted here. You must have this book. Set it next to Matt Trewhella's Doctrine of the Lesser Magistrate and refer to both. Often."
—Rev. Jon Speed Pastor, Christ is King Baptist Church Co-Producer, *Babies Are Murdered Here*

"With the surgical precision of a writer's scalpel, Cali relentlessly cuts away at the irrational inconsistency of many secular pro-life arguments, arguments which often end up doing more harm than good, because of their logical duplicity for the sake of political victories and long term strategies. Agree with him or every point or not, it is important that pro-life Christians understand the inconsistencies inherent in the broader pro-life movement if we want to truly see the abomination of abortion come to an end."
—Doug Van Dorn, Pastor of Reformed Baptist Church of Northern Colorado

"Pastor Cali has written a bracing book. He is clear, decisive, focused and forceful in his argument that Christians should take our marching orders from the written Word of God rather than the secular culture when we think about and respond to the abortion holocaust that plagues America. While there is room for debate over strategies (for example, principled incrementalism vs. abolitionism), Cali helps mark out in no uncertain terms the biblical foundation and parameters that should govern such debate. Abortion is murder and should be fought against as such. There are only three kinds of people who should read this book: Christians who have been actively involved in the pro-life movement; Christians who have not been involved in the pro-life movement; and those who are not Christians."
—Tom Ascol, Pastor of Grace Baptist Church, President of Founders Ministries

"My friend CR Cali has given the church a formidable weapon in its fight with abortion. This little book is a loud and clear trumpet to wake the drowsy citizens of Christ's kingdom, a very sledgehammer of biblical truth and plain reason. If readers think the author has gone Martin Luther at times, let them be thankful that it is Luther and not Melanchthon. The hour calls for Luther."
—Luke Walker, Pastor of Redeeming Cross Community Church, Minneapolis. Author, *Lemuel Haynes: The Black Puritan*, *Martin Luther: The Iron Pen*

THE DOCTRINE OF BALAAM

THE DOCTRINE OF BALAAM

A polemic against the secular Pro-life establishment, and an exhortation with encouragement to the persecuted bride of Christ to resist the temptation of fellowship with darkness; nor yoke themselves with the course of this world; nor whore themselves out to the prince of the power of the air, who is full of the accusation "Did God really say?"; and to flee seeking carnal goals and pragmatic means of compromise towards them rather than obedience to the word of God and trust in His sovereign control and care through providence, responding rightly with our Lord as He rebuked the enemy of God with, "Thus, says the Lord," as it relates in particular to the Christian response to the murder of preborn children.

by

CR Cali

WRATH AND GRACE PUBLISHING

COLUMBUS, GA

This book is dedicated to Cheryl. As unregenerate best friends for a decade, you stood by me. Since the time that God saved you, you have not ceased to pray for me, encourage me, and walk with me in the Lord.

And to all the Christians that boldly shared the gospel with me as I mocked you to your face in the vilest ways. I thank God for the courageous stance you took and the love you showed in your oppression. May God grant us the strength to rest in His power.

TABLE OF CONTENTS

INTRODUCTION

By way of introduction, I would like to explain why I am writing this book, as well as its outline. My prayer is that you are edified by its content, encouraged to examine the Scriptures, and moved to action. I welcome honest dialog as we come to sharpen each other.

WHY I AM WRITING THIS BOOK

As a pagan, I was quite vocal in my hostility toward God. This was often expressed in my general disdain for those created in His image, and, in particular, disgust for those I thought were useless to me as a resource. I was outspoken in favor of eugenics and abortion advocacy. But God pulled me out of this hateful rebellion by His grace. He changed my heart to love Him and men. He changed my mind, giving me Christ's. Being a young and immature Christian, I did not have a developed understanding of the image of God in relation to abortion. I knew abortion was wrong, and that I was now against it. I was a Christian, so I was Pro-Life (but I didn't really know what it meant). That was as far as I got for quite some time. When the question of abortion came up, I regurgitated the secular Pro-Life position. I assumed its synonymy with the Christian position. I notice the same confusion whenever I engage professing (and well-meaning) Christians on the topic of abortion, and my experience is borne out by the research. A 2017 Pew Research Center poll of public opinion on abortion shows that 29% of white evangelical protestants and 55% of black evangelical protestants believe that abortion should be legal in all or most cases. Setting aside for now the racial disparity, the numbers reveal a problem in the church. Her members do not view the murder of preborn children rightly.

For now, let's focus on the 70% and 41% who believe abortion should be illegal in all or most cases. In 2016, Barna conducted a similar poll with the same results. Only 13% of professing Christians believed that abortion should be illegal in all cases, and 75 percent thought it should be regulated through the first trimester. These recent polls show that the secular Pro-Life establishment, their ideology and methodology, has infiltrated the church. The biblical position is the minority position among professing believers, and many Christians believe what the world has to say over and against what God has said. Unknowingly, professing Christians have come to believe that the secular Pro-Life position *is* the Christian position.

ORGANIZATION AND OUTLINE OF THIS BOOK

The first chapter will deal with the theological framework used to discuss this issue. This chapter will lay the groundwork and building blocks that will be used in the rest of the book. In it we will define the image of God, its corruption in the fall, and its restoration in union with Christ. Here we will encounter the accusation of the serpent, which has become the battle cry of the world against our Creator, as well as the only reasonable response to such an accusation. The text of Scripture will warn us that the church has been infiltrated by worldly wisdom, ideology, and methodology; it will then call us to repent and stand firm. We will demonstrate that the secular Pro-Life establishment has been a greater influence on the thinking of professing Christians than the word of God.

The following chapters will examine several key positions held by the secular Pro-Life establishment. We will see whether they align with what God has said or follow after the course of this world and the prince of the power of the air. The Second victim or Equal Justice chapter will look at the secular Pro-Life establishment's unyielding position that parents—especially mothers—are not to be considered perpetrators in the act of abortion and should be exempt from prosecution. The chapter Iniquitous Decrees and Calling Evil Good will examine the laws written by the secular Pro-Life establishment. We will make explicit and implicit readings of these laws that sanction and regulate the murder of preborn children. Can someone with the mind of Christ support such laws in good conscience and call them good? The chapter Doctrine of Lesser Magistrate: Defy Tyrants will consider civil idolatry, in particular the secular Pro-Life movement's faith in the supreme court (SCOTUS), and the biblical doctrine of the lesser magistrate, which stands in direct contradistinction to the former. The chapter People of Providence: Different Metric for Success will look at the stated goal of the secular Pro-Life movement, and the carnal means of compromise they employ to achieve these carnal ends. This will be juxtaposed with a call to obedience and trust in the God of providence. We will finally look into a variety of activities that Christians can involve themselves in as they engage the culture of death.

Whenever possible I will quote leaders of secular Pro-Life organizations to lay out in their own words the doctrinal positions we are examining. I will start the refutation of the secular Pro-Life doctrine using general revelation to expose the inconsistency and impotence of their claims. Then, with the text of Scripture, we will prove that the secular Pro-Life doctrine runs counter to our Christian faith.

The reader will notice the repeated use of the phrase secular Pro-Life. The term secular *when added to Pro-Life is to expose, as is the purpose of this book, the doctrine and methodology as being of the world and not found in the text of Scripture. As we will see, there are many respectable Christians that hold to this secular Pro-Life doctrine and dress it up in Christian terminology. This by no means makes them not Christian. It does however show the inconsistency in applying the truth of God's word to this issue. My hope in showing the distinguishing marks that separate the secular Pro-life doctrine from Christian doctrine is that we all can continue to be conformed to Christ and His word.*

THE PURPOSE OF THIS BOOK

The purpose of this polemic against the secular Pro-Life establishment is to expose it as antichristian. I want to be clear from the onset that I am talking about the ideology and methodology that drives the secular Pro-Life establishment positions and not the people themselves. This is not an attack on the movement's leaders nor anyone that holds to their positions. It is meant to focus on the doctrinal statements themselves and show that they do not reflect what God has said. My hope is that professing Christians will see this discrepancy and go to the text of Scripture to verify what is asserted in this book. My purpose in writing is to call Christians to repent and take on the mind of Christ that we, as redeemed saints, all possess. It is to remind us all, that the holy Scripture is the only sufficient, certain, and infallible rule of all saving knowledge, faith, and obedience. God has spoken to us all, through the text of Scripture, on every aspect of our lives as Christians. I hope this book encourages and convicts you.

DOCTRINE OF BALAAM

"And to the angel of the church in Pergamum write: The One who has the sharp two-edged sword says this: 'I know where you dwell, where Satan's throne is; and you hold fast My name, and did not deny My faith even in the days of Antipas, My witness, My faithful one, who was killed among you, where Satan dwells. 'But I have a few things against you, because you have there some who hold the teaching of Balaam, who kept teaching Balak to put a stumbling block before the sons of Israel, to eat things sacrificed to idols and to commit acts of immorality. 'So you also have some who in the same way hold the teaching of the Nicolaitans. 'Therefore repent; or else I am coming to you quickly, and I will make war against them with the sword of My mouth. 'He who has an ear, let him hear what the Spirit says to the churches. To him who overcomes, to him I will give some of the hidden manna, and I will give him a white stone, and a new name written on the stone which no one knows but he who receives it." — *Revelation 2:12-17*

The doctrine of Balaam will be the foundation of our discussion of abortion and the church's biblical response. In this chapter we will explain what it is, its errors, and its danger. This illustration, given to us by our Lord, builds a framework that accurately describes the current condition of professing Christians and their relationship with the secular Pro-Life establishment. It is with this framework in mind that we will compare the biblical position with the secular Pro-Life position. For this reason, we will spend a considerable amount of space outlining a biblically accurate template with which to judge our current condition. As we move forward, we will refer to the building blocks laid out in this chapter. My hope is that this dominical exhortation pushes us to reformation, retrieval, and revival of biblical doctrine and its appropriate application. My prayer is that we heed God's call for us to repent.[1]

---

[1] When our Lord and Master Jesus Christ said "Repent," he intended that the entire life of believers should be repentance. This was the first of Luther's 95 theses nailed to the door of Castel Church in Wittenburg on 31 October, 1517. Let us be mindful of the work of our Lord in maturing His bride, that we may not be tossed to and fro by every wind of doctrine. This happens through the ordinary means of grace, primarily through the word of God. Luther reminds us of the active role of God in our repentance... "Now this is the thunderbolt of God, by means of which he destroys both the open sinner and the false saint and allows no one to be right" ...this is not "active contrition," a contrived remorse, but "passive contrition," true affliction of the heart, suffering, and the pain of death. (Martin Luther, "The Smalcald Articles" in *Martin Luther's Basic Theological Writings* [Minneapolis: Fortress Press, 2012], 352). It is God acting upon His children; molding them; refining them; purifying them; giving to them faith. "Therefore, just as the Holy Spirit says,"today if you hear his voice, do not harden your hearts as when they provoked me,as in the day of trial in the wilderness, where your fathers tried me by testing me,and saw my works for forty years. 'therefore i was angry with this generation, and said, "they always go astray in their heart, and they did not know my ways" ; as I swore in my wrath, 'they shall not enter my rest.'"

FEAR NOT, I AM WITH YOU

To give a robust understanding of the dangers of the doctrine of Balaam, we must see it in the context of the entirety of Scripture. God concludes His special revelation with the Revelation of Jesus Christ, the faithful witness, the firstborn of the dead, the ruler of kings on earth. It is here that God ordained an opportunity to encourage His persecuted church in her time of purification and maturation. God has given us this comforting phrase as an expression of preservation through His works as Creator and as Redeemer.

God finished His works of creation and entered His rest, ruling and reigning as Sovereign, upholding the universe by the word of His power, being intimately involved in enforcing the laws that He instituted through His creative action.[2] We

---

[2] All mankind is created in the image of God, and because of that, His invisible attributes, His eternal power and divine nature, have been clearly seen, being understood through what has been made. We look out at creation and God is revealed to us. In creation Christ the perfect law giver institutes among other things physical laws of nature, and binds His creation to them. Speed of light or sound, laws of motion, and universal law of gravity would be a few examples. To this day, if I raise a book and let go it will fall to the ground. In a very real sense this is our Lord perfectly enforcing the laws of physics that he established in creation. Our God, the Creator, is intimately involved with His creation. He perfectly executes judgment and enforces His laws, keeping order by upholding the universe by the word of His power. This illustration typifies the moral law of God that He has established in creating man in His image. We should see the perfect law giver and law enforcer. We should be reminded of the words of Abraham "Far be it from You to do such a thing, to slay the righteous with the wicked, so that the righteous and the wicked are treated alike. Far be it from You! Shall not the Judge of all the earth deal justly?" He will not turn a blind eye to sin. He will by no means leave *the guilty* unpunished. Yet, The Lord, the Lord God, compassionate and gracious, slow to anger, and abounding in lovingkindness and truth; who keeps lovingkindness for thousands, who forgives iniquity, transgression

call this the work of God in providence, which may be described in this way: God the good Creator of all things, in his infinite power and wisdom doth uphold, direct, dispose, and govern all creatures and things, from the greatest even to the least, by his most wise and holy providence, to the end for the which they were created, according unto his infallible foreknowledge, and the free and immutable counsel of his own will; to the praise of the glory of his wisdom, power, justice, infinite goodness, and mercy.[3]

To this day when it rains, we look out and see a rainbow and cannot help but think of the works of God in providence and common preservation, remembering the established covenant imposed by God on Noah, his offspring, all the flesh on the earth, and all the living creatures. God says in Genesis 8:22, "While the earth remains, seedtime and harvest, and cold and heat, and summer and winter, and day and night, shall not cease." Through providence our Creator is directing, disposing, and governing all creatures and things. In this, He is preserving creation and moving history forward by His ultimate care and control until the day of the Lord, which day the execution of judgment in the flood narrative typified. The governance of God through common preservation in providence determines all of the circumstances of history, to

---

and sin. The just Judge enforces His laws by punishing the innocent God-Man in the place of sinners. It pleased the Father to crush His Son as He poured out the wrath due His children as He executed the judgment they deserve. I would urge you to make a conscious effort to recognize the perfection of our Creator as He reveals Himself in His creation and give Him the honor, thanksgiving and acknowledgment He is owed. Let that be a reminder to you, beloved, of our Redeemer as He reveals Himself in Scripture and give Him the worship He is due, in Spirit and in Truth.

[3] Second London Baptist Confession of Faith, 5.1.

His glory, in which all of the elect are born, regenerated and sanctified, and all of the reprobate are born and fill their cup of wrath.

Seventeenth-century particular Baptists noted: As the providence of God doth in general reach to all creatures, so after a more special manner it taketh care of his church, and disposeth of all things to the good thereof.[4] Here in this affirmation we, as the body of Christ, find encouragement in the circumstance ordained by our Sovereign Creator and Redeemer. The care and governing control of God directing history is how He in His infinite wisdom chose to establish, build, and sanctify His church. It is through His works of providence that the church is not only being preserved, but being made ready to be presented before Him, blameless and spotless. The promised persecution of the church is God actively pruning, refining, cleansing, and purging her, and it is under His control and direction, according to the counsel of His good pleasure. Our King, the faithful witness, comforts us in the midst of trials and persecution by reminding us that He, the One that is directing, disposing, and governing all creatures and things, is in our midst.

As partners in the tribulation and the kingdom and the patient endurance that are in Jesus, let us find comfort in Him,[5] in His works of providence and redemption, and in His

---

[4] Second London Baptist Confession of Faith, 5.7.

[5] I find myself coming back to the words of the Orthodox Catechism. I am reminded through this exposition of the power and glory of our Lord and the joy and comfort that we have in Him.

words to us as the thematic focus of the Revelation of Jesus Christ, saying, "Fear not, I am the first and the last, and the living one. I died, and behold I am alive forevermore, and I have the keys of Death and Hades."[6]

SHARP TWO-EDGED SWORD AND THE IMAGE OF GOD

Our Lord speaks to His children words of encouragement and exhortation in the Revelation of Jesus Christ by pointing to Himself, disclosing His attributes, works, purpose, and plan. We are examining what He says about these things in Revelation 2:12-17. He bookends this section of commendation, condemnation, and call to repentance with an allusion to the sharp two-edged sword proceeding from His mouth. In his commentary on the book of Revelation, G.K. Beale rightly says, "Again, Christ introduces Himself with one of His descriptions from the ch. 1 vision, which is uniquely appropriate for the situation of this church. The depiction dominates the literary framework of the letter, since the same image from 1:16 also forms the conclusion to the letter (2:16). Therefore, Christ standing over the church as

---

Q1. What is your only comfort in life and death? A. That I am not my own, but belong with body and soul, both in life and in death, to my faithful Saviour Jesus Christ. He has fully paid for all my sins with his precious blood, and has set me free from all the power of the devil. He also preserves me in such a way that without the will of my heavenly Father not a hair can fall from my head; indeed, all things must work together for my salvation. Therefore, by his Holy Spirit he also assures me of eternal life and makes me heartily willing and ready from now on to live for him.

[6] Revelation 1:17-18 (ESV).

a threatening judge because of the church's sin is the thought pervading the entire epistle to Pergamum."[7]

This two-edged sword from the mouth of our Lord is the standard by which judgment is made;[8] it is universal, unchanging and, as Isaiah tells us, will stand forever as it judges with perfection. As we shall see, this standard which we will be judged by is also the very standard we are commanded to use in our judgments as image bearers. God has given us this standard as He has revealed Himself to us in the light of nature, and more clearly in holy Scripture, and ultimately in the person of the Son, our Lord Jesus Christ. Let us not forget that these two types of revelation, general revelation and special revelation, are making known the same God and the same standards of righteousness.

In His acts of creation and providence, God reveals His eternal power and divine nature. We see the perfect lawgiver and the perfect law enforcer. Ever since the creation of the world God has been clearly perceived by all men because we are all created in the image of God. Contained in that image is the moral law of God, which is also called natural law.[9] As

---

[7] G.K.Beale, *The New International Greek Testament Commentary the Book of Revelation* (Grand Rapids: Wm. B. Eerdmans Publishing Co., 1999), 245-46.

[8] Hebrews 4:11-13 reads, "Therefore let us be diligent to enter that rest, so that no one will fall, through following the same example of disobedience. For the word of God is living and active and sharper than any two-edged sword, and piercing as far as the division of soul and spirit, of both joints and marrow, and able to judge the thoughts and intentions of the heart. And there is no creature hidden from His sight, but all things are open and laid bare to the eyes of Him with whom we have to do."

[9] The following books, both by Dr. David VanDrunen, give great detail to moral law, natural law, and the image of God. *Divine Covenants and Moral Order: A Biblical Theology of Natural Law* and *Natural Law and the Two Kingdoms: A Study in the Development of Reformed Social Thought.*

the Sovereign Creator, God is due perfect obedience from His creatures. In fact, He demands it. In His infinite wisdom, He endows those that bear His image with the very standard they must meet.

Obedience is just another way of talking about judgments being put into action. Man's obedience to the moral law of God is man making judgments using that moral law as the standard, plumb line, or rule. "Positive actings must have positive precepts," says John Owen.[10] Adam, the prototypal created son of God was made upright and righteous. Thematically, sonship[11] is about obedience and proper judgment. Being made in the image of God, man was given the priestly duty to "cultivate and keep" the garden temple where God dwelt with man.[12] This charge to cultivate and

---

[10] John Owen, *Works*, (Edinburgh: Banner of Truth, 2009) 8.164.

[11] In short, we see Adam the created son of God (Luke 3:38). This sonship is tied to the image and likeness in which Adam is created, and in part to the judgments made from the standard in that image and likeness. Adam's disobedience is contrasted in the movement from Luke 3:38 into Luke 4 and the obedience of our Lord, the only begotten Son. There is a recapitulation of Adam, the covenant breaking disobedient son, to be found in the nation of Israel that God calls His first-born son. Christians being conformed to the image of the Son by the renewing of our minds are adopted sons performing gospel obedience. Brandon Crowe's dissertation *The Obedient Son: Deuteronomy and Christology in the Gospel of Matthew* is a very helpful read. It is out of print but can be found digitally on Logos. A more accessible book by the same author is *The Last Adam: A Theology of the Obedient Life of Jesus in the Gospels.*

[12] I have found the following resources to be valuable on this topic. T. Desmod Alexander, *From Eden to the New Jerusalem: An Introduction to Biblical Theology*; Richard C. Barcellos, *Better Than the Beginning: Creation in Biblical Perspective*; Richard C. Barcellos, *Getting the Garden Right: Adam's Work and God's Rest in Light of Christ*; G. K. Beale, *God Dwells Among Us: Expanding Eden to the Ends of the Earth*; G. K. Beale, *The Temple and the Church's Mission: A Biblical Theology of the Dwelling Place of God*; Stephen G.

keep is also expressed in the commands by God to "rule over," "be fruitful and multiply," and "subdue." They are each connected to man being created in God's image and according to His likeness. In other words, dominion, subduing, and obedience are the positive actions of judging based on the moral law given to us. Being fruitful and multiplying—filling the earth with sinless image bearers that go and do likewise—was to be the cultivation and expansion of that temple where He was God to them, and they His people.

Adam functions as a prototypal priest-judge in Eden in his service to God. In much the same way, the cherubim with the flaming sword take over that function after the fall and expulsion, and subsequently, the priests in their service to the tabernacle and temple for the nation of Israel. They were to defend the borders of this holy communion with God. Their charge was to judge all impropriety and lack of conformity to the standard set by God the perfect lawgiver. To do so, they were armed with that two-edged sword proceeding from the mouth of our Lord. This, in part, is what it means to image God.[13]

Dempster, *Dominion and Dynasty: A Theology of the Hebrew Bible*; W. J. Dumbrell, *The End of the Beginning: Revelation 21-22 and the Old Testament*; J. V. Fesko, *Death in Adam, Life in Christ: The Doctrine of Imputation* (Reformed Exegetical Doctrinal Studies series); J. V. Fesko, *Last Things First: Unlocking Genesis with the Christ of Eschatology*; Meredith G. Kline, *God, Heaven, and Har Magedon: A Covenantal Tale of Cosmos and Telos*; Meredith G. Kline, *Images of the Spirit*; Meredith G. Kline, *Kingdom Prologue: Genesis Foundations for a Covenantal Worldview*; Oren Martin, *Bound for the Promised Land*.

[13] Timothy Brindle does a great job describing the biblical theology of priest/judge in connection to the duties of God's image bearers in the song Priest-Judge off the Unfolding album. *https://www.youtube.com/watch?v=DR8kolGfTY4*.

The craftiest beast enters this holy habitation and the first recorded words of his mouth are "did God really say...?" This has become the rally cry of the world in its rebellion against God. They now rage and plot in vain against Him and His rightful rule and reign as the Sovereign Creator. This was the proving grounds for Adam, and by covenantal extension, all his offspring. With the truth of God's word at his disposal, he surrendered his duty to execute justice in allegiance to and on behalf of his Creator. He did not put God's enemy under foot and decapitate him with that fierce blade of living truth. Neglecting his priestly duties and authority (by not standing on the word of God), Adam fell prey to the temptation and accusation against the veracity of God and His word. This manifests the ultimate miscarriage of justice, as Adam failed to image God properly by responding in the only appropriate manner, *Thus says the Lord.*

Adam's disobedience is a failure to image God in guarding the holiness of God's temple from the unclean beast and executing judgment against him. This marred the image of God in all his offspring. They all willingly join in his rebellion, doing what is right in their own eyes. All of mankind are children of wrath and born hostile to God, not submitting to His laws. Indeed they cannot. The moral law in the image of God strips man of any excuse. As they suppress that truth in unrighteousness and continue to judge improperly, their corruption is expressed. They are all fools. They say in their hearts that there is no God, and they live their lives for themselves, following the course of this world and the prince of the power of the air, indulging in the desires of their flesh and mind. Their seditious outcry is, "Let us tear their fetters apart and cast away their cords from us!"[14] Through Adam there is a world full of image bearers that are corrupted to the core, accusing God and justifying their treason with the very words of the serpent, *Did God really say?*

But God, being rich in mercy, because of His great love with which He loved us, sent the Eternal Son of God, who is the radiance of His glory and the exact representation of His nature. Our Lord, the last Adam, took on flesh and successfully imaged God where the first Adam failed. He lived a representative life of perfect obedience for His children, judging with precision according to God's standard. When He was faced with the same accusation from the devil, "Did God really say?" Christ responded promptly in a judicious and priestly manner with, "Thus says the Lord." His obedience led Him to the cross where He took on the sins of all those that would come to Him; it pleased the Father to crush Him in the place of all those He gives to the Eternal Begotten Son as a people. The full measure of wrath, deserved by His children, was poured out on the innocent God-Man. Judgment for the sins against His Sovereign rule and reign was paid by our King. He passed through the flaming sword of judgment on our behalf. He rose from the dead, resurrected to sit on His throne, high and

---

[14] Psalm 2:3.

lifted up.[15] On that cross victorious, He executed judgment on the serpent, crushing his head. I urge you to look to the cross and see your sins there; take for yourself the righteousness that He earned; be crushed by the power of the word that proceeds from His mouth and surrender. These are the terms of peace.

"Comfort, O comfort My people," says your God. "Speak kindly to Jerusalem; And call out to her, that her warfare has ended, That her iniquity has been removed, That she has received of the Lord's hand Double for all her sins."[16]

He that is united to Christ in His life, death, and resurrection is given His mind. By the mercies of God, you are being transformed into the image of the Son by the renewing of your mind. The curse of the corrupted image is being restored. You are freed not only from the penalty of your sin,

---

[15] The theme of the exaltation of the suffering servant is a prominent and beautiful one. In John 3:12-18, Jesus masterfully points out this theme by showing the connection of Daniel 7, Isaiah 6, and Numbers 21 as they typify the person and work of our Lord in redeeming a people, and the path they must follow in their purification and maturation. The theme of Job and Isaiah bring this to the forefront. The lives of the prophets, Joseph, Abraham, Job, etc. all point to the Seed of the woman with a bruised heel that crushes the head of the serpent, then sits enthroned, entering God's rest. It is the pattern followed by the apostles and martyrs of the church and all that are joined to our Lord and King, who for the joy set before Him endured the cross, despising the shame, sat down at the right hand of the throne of God. See John Owen vol. 1, Luke Walker *Have You Considered My Servant Job?* (forthcoming), Voddie Baucham *Joseph and the Gospel of Many Colors*, Ben Witherington III *Isaiah Old and New: Exegesis, Intertextuality, and Hermeneutics*, Michael Rydelnik *Messianic Hope*. Timothy Brindle's song Wilderness off the Unfolding album is very good also.

[16] Isaiah 40:1-2.

but from your slavery to it. You are an adopted son of the Most High, with all the rights, privileges, and responsibilities of a son. As a priest in His kingdom, you now have the right, duty, and mind to serve the true temple. You are given the charge to cultivate and keep that holy communion by proper judgment with the two-edged sword as you, by faith, image God appropriately, purging the sin within. With the restored image, and word of God to stand on in confidence, Christians can respond to the world's rebellious accusations of *Did God really say?* as Christ did, with *Thus says the Lord.*[17]

---

[17] The last three paragraphs of chapter 19 of the Second London Baptist Confession of Faith (quoted below) explain the interaction of the believer, under grace, with the law of God. We have gospel obedience in union with Christ.

> The moral law doth for ever bind all, as well justified persons as others, to the obedience thereof, and that not only in regard of the matter contained in it, but also in respect of the authority of God the Creator, who gave it; neither doth Christ in the Gospel any way dissolve, but much strengthen this obligation.
>
> Although true believers be not under the law as a covenant of works, to be thereby justified or condemned, yet it is of great use to them as well as to others, in that as a rule of life, informing them of the will of God and their duty, it directs and binds them to walk accordingly; discovering also the sinful pollutions of their natures, hearts, and lives, so as examining themselves thereby, they may come to further conviction of, humiliation for, and hatred against, sin; together with a clearer sight of the need they have of Christ and the perfection of his obedience; it is likewise of use to the regenerate to restrain their corruptions, in that it forbids sin; and the threatenings of it serve to shew what even their sins deserve, and what afflictions in this life they may expect for them, although freed from the curse and unallayed rigour thereof. The promises of it likewise shew them God's approbation of obedience, and what blessings they may expect upon the performance thereof, though not as due to them by the law as a covenant of works; so as man's doing good and refraining from evil, because the law encourageth to the one and deterreth from the other, is no evidence of his being under the law and not under grace.

WHERE SATAN'S THRONE IS; AND YOU HOLD FAST MY NAME

Our Lord Jesus Christ commends the church in Pergamum with an interesting construction of phrases. "I know where you dwell, where Satan's throne is; and you hold fast My name, and did not deny My faith..." Jesus is reminding His people that, by His providence, the field of this world contains both wheat and tare; regenerate, born again believers in union with Him and unregenerate God-haters united to Adam's rebellion; or, restored priestly image bearers that correctly judge with, "Thus says the Lord," and corrupted image bearers that judge selfishly, justifying their treasonous sin with, "Did God really say?"

God saves sinners and changes their hearts and minds. This does not mean there is a change in vocation, marital status, or national citizenship. What it does mean is that the Christian can approach these, and all cultural activities, with the mind of Christ. They will judge properly with the word of God as they endeavor these activities, bringing the gospel into conflict with the corruption found in the world. As a new creature, you can excel vocationally, you can far surpass any worldly standard for being a spouse, and you can be the best model citizen. You have this ability because you do these things unto the Lord, by His power and with His mind, standing on the truth of His word. When God redeems us out

---

Neither are the aforementioned uses of the law contrary to the grace of the Gospel, but do sweetly comply with it, the Spirit of Christ subduing and enabling the will of man to do that freely and cheerfully which the will of God, revealed in the law, requireth to be done.

of this worldwide system of defiance and rebellion, He leaves us here on His earth as regenerate priests in the kingdom of God to navigate through this common kingdom, performing our priestly duties in service to His true temple. In His high priestly prayer, Jesus says it like this:

> But now I come to You; and these things I speak in the world so that they may have My joy made full in themselves. I have given them Your word; and the world has hated them, because they are not of the world, even as I am not of the world. I do not ask You to take them out of the world, but to keep them from the evil one. They are not of the world, even as I am not of the world. Sanctify them in the truth; Your word is truth. As You sent Me into the world, I also have sent them into the world. For their sakes I sanctify Myself, that they themselves also may be sanctified in truth.
>
> I do not ask on behalf of these alone, but for those also who believe in Me through their word; that they may all be one; even as You, Father, are in Me and I in You, that they also may be in Us, so that the world may believe that You sent Me. (John 17:13-21).

The commendation from our Lord in Revelation 2:13 is an acknowledgment that the redeemed saints profess the name of Christ and do not deny Him as they live side-by-side with unbelievers, even being persecuted by them in this common kingdom. He is reminding His church that they have the mind of Christ, His word as their sword, and are to use it to judge, saying, "Thus says the Lord," as they live among a world of corrupted image bearers that suppress the truth with their unrighteousness and try to justify their sin with the accusation of, "Did God really say?"

THE TEACHING OF BALAAM AND NUMBERS 31:16

Jesus continues with an indictment in Revelation 2:14, "But I have a few things against you, because you have there some who hold the teaching of Balaam, who kept teaching Balak to put a stumbling block before the sons of Israel, to eat things sacrificed to idols and to commit *acts of* immorality."

Following in Adam's footsteps, the physical seed of Abraham, the nation of Israel, was also a disobedient son. In fact, God calls Israel His first-born son who ,like Adam, broke covenant with Him. They were commanded to image God as His son and bring His judgment to the land of promise, dispossessing its idolatrous inhabitants. God had devoted His enemies to destruction; His first-born son, His people, His nation of priests, was to purge the land of sin. They were warned not to intermarry or have fellowship with those pagan God-haters, forbidden to be unequally yoked to them and their evil practices. They were to execute justice for God, and, with their feet on the necks of God's enemies, crush them. God exhorted them not to take wives and plunder from the conquest, lest they become like them.

> Moses and Eleazar the priest and all the leaders of the congregation went out to meet them outside the camp. Moses was angry with the officers of the army, the captains of thousands and the captains of

> hundreds, who had come from service in the war. And Moses said to them, "Have you spared all the women? Behold, these caused the sons of Israel, through the counsel of Balaam, to trespass against the Lord in the matter of Peor, so the plague was among the congregation of the Lord (Numbers 31:13-16).

The physical seed of Abraham, God's first-born son, disobeyed on the Canaanite conquest and followed the counsel of Balaam, which declared the words of the ancient serpent, "Did God really say?" In doing so they strayed from their charge and, like Adam, rebelled against their God. They failed to respond in the only proper way, "Thus says the Lord." Rather than communing with God and defending the holiness of this temple with the sword of the truth, the word of God, they participated in idolatry. They were an adulterous people, defiling the land by becoming like the people they were to dispossess.

In Revelation 2:14 our Lord is exposing the sin of His people, the spiritual seed of Abraham, by pointing them to the example of the physical seed of Abraham. Paul gives the same warning to the church in 1 Corinthians 10:11, "Now these things happened to them as an example, and they were written for our instruction, upon whom the ends of the ages have come." The sojourning of the physical seed of Abraham, including their following the counsel of Balaam, actually happened in time and space. This was a real event which was intended by God's providence to be an example, or type. It illustrates something about the spiritual sojourning of the spiritual seed of Abraham, or the church. We know this because God says it was written for our instruction.

This indictment reminds us that while we live in this world, we are not to follow the course of this world. We are not to have fellowship or communion with them and their evil practices. We must not be unequally yoked with them, their worldly wisdom, their methodology, their underhanded schemes, and their carnality. We are to participate in culture with the mind of Christ as priests in His kingdom, standing on the word of God and saying, "Thus says the Lord," rather than listening to the counsel of Balaam and joining with the world that declares, "Did God really say?" In this we are to obey God and trust in His providence.

Here is a call to repent, lest that same sword of truth by which we are to judge is turned against us in war. We are reminded that we have the mind of Christ, that we are priests in His kingdom and are armed with the sword of truth. We are called adopted sons that have Christ's righteousness and are being transformed into His image. Therefore, we are to be obedient and imitate the Eternal Begotten Son in whom the Father is well pleased by standing firm on His word. We are to turn from our idolatry and the disobedience displayed in Adam, the created son of God, and in Israel the first-born son.

HE WHO HAS AN EAR, LET HIM HEAR

Revelation 2:17 begins with a command from our Lord to His people, one that follows His pattern of words used in creation. Because of the noetic effects of the fall on the corrupted image of God,[18] our ability to hear his word requires a sovereign act of God. We keep on listening but do not perceive; we keep on looking but do not understand. Our hearts have been rendered insensitive, our ears dull, our eyes dim. This allusion to the prophecy of Isaiah 6 and its solution is used through the entirety of Scripture. Paul further details this problem and God's solution in 1 Corinthians 1:10-16:

> For to us God revealed *them* through the Spirit; for the Spirit searches all things, even the depths of God. For who among men knows the *thoughts* of a man except the spirit of the man which is in him? Even so the *thoughts* of God no one knows except the Spirit of God. Now we have received, not the spirit of the world, but the Spirit who is from God, so that we may know the things freely given to us by God, which things we also speak, not in words taught by human wisdom, but in those taught by the Spirit, combining spiritual *thoughts* with spiritual *words*. But a natural man does not accept the things of the Spirit of God, for they are foolishness to him; and he cannot understand them, because they are spiritually appraised. But he who is spiritual appraises all things, yet he himself is appraised by no one. For who has known the mind of the Lord, that

[18]In general, we are referring to sin's corrupting effect on the intellect. As we mentioned earlier, the image of God that all mankind bears has been radically corrupted by sin entering the world through Adam. We are dealing, in particular, with improper desires and failing ability to process our knowledge of our Creator. Arguably, this has implications to our understanding of creation that reveals its Creator.

he will instruct Him? But we have the mind of Christ. (1 Corinthians 1:10-16).

Christian, you have the mind of Christ, and you have the Spirit to instruct you and illuminate His words to you. Unregenerate man has only his corrupted image to rely upon and he will not accept what the Spirit says. Your ears have been opened to hear Him; theirs remain dull. Jesus says to the unregenerate Jews in John 10:25-27, "I told you, and you do not believe; the works that I do in My Father's name, these testify of Me. But you do not believe because you are not of My sheep. My sheep hear My voice, and I know them, and they follow Me." Earlier He said, "To him the doorkeeper opens, and the sheep hear his voice, and he calls his own sheep by name and leads them out. When he puts forth all his own, he goes ahead of them, and the sheep follow him because they know his voice. A stranger they simply will not follow, but will flee from him, because they do not know the voice of strangers" (John 10:3-5).

CONCLUSION

My assertion is that the professing Christian's relationship with the secular Pro-Life establishment is following the counsel of Balaam, and that Jesus calls us to repent. I will spend the rest of this book examining the ideology and methodology of the secular Pro-Life industry establishment, and the disastrous effect it has had on the Christian. Secular Pro-Life ideology and methodology have infiltrated the church of Jesus Christ. Many of her members hold fast to the name of Christ and have not denied His faith, but hold the doctrine of Balaam by marrying themselves to this secular ideology. Beloved, we have the mind of Christ and His Spirit. As we carefully look at these secular Pro-Life establishment doctrinal positions, we will ask which category they fall into: "Did God really say?" or "Thus says the Lord." May God grant us repentance.

SECOND VICTIM OR EQUAL JUSTICE

In this chapter we will consider one of the secular Pro-Life establishment's uncompromising doctrinal pillars: *treating the abortive mother as the second victim* in abortion. We will expose the inconsistency of their argumentation by refuting each point in turn and conclude by contrasting this position with what God has said about equal justice.

Simply put, this doctrine states that women who murder their preborn children by way of abortion should not be considered perpetrators in this crime, but rather should be thought of as second victims in the crime of abortion. The arguments against subjecting abortive mothers to equal justice fall under three major points: Indoctrination, Coercion/Duress, and Proximate Justice/lack of effectiveness. We will begin by looking at several recent quotes from Pro-Life industry and organization leaders showing their continual support and propagation of this doctrine.

National Right to Life President Carol Tobias in a 30 March 2016 press release:

> The National Right to Life Committee unequivocally opposes the killing of innocent unborn children and works unceasingly to have them protected in law.

> Unborn children and their mothers are victims in an abortion. In adopting statutes prohibiting the performance of abortions, National Right to Life has long opposed the imposition of penalties on the woman on whom an abortion is attempted or performed.[19]

March for Life Education and Defense Fund President Jeanne Mancini in a 30 March 2016 press release:

> No pro-lifer would ever want to punish a woman who has chosen abortion... This is against the very nature of what we are about.... We invite a woman who has gone down this route to consider paths to healing, not punishment...[20]

Susan B. Anthony List President Marjorie Dannenfelser in a 30 March 2016 press release:

> But let us be clear: punishment is solely for the abortionist who profits off of the destruction of one life and the grave wounding of another...We have never advocated, in any context, for the punishment of women who undergo abortion. [21]

Operation Rescue's Troy Newman told *LifeSiteNews* in October 2014:

---

[19]https://www.nrlc.org/site/communications/releases/2016/release033016b/.
[20] http://marchforlife.org/no-pro-life-american/.
[21] https://www.sba-list.org/home/sba-list-trumps-abortion-comments.

> It is far outside the mainstream of pro-life thought to suggest that women who have abortions deserve capital punishment. Pro-life activists have compassion for women, who are often pressured into having abortions they don't really want...The pro-life movement considers the woman the secondary victim in abortion... The true culprits that deserve to suffer criminal punishments are the abortionists, who prey on vulnerable women and profit from their suffering.[22]

Founder of And Then There Were None, Abby Johnson, told *LifeSiteNews* in October 2014:

> As pro-lifers, we must preach mercy, not condemnation. We believe that abortion is the ultimate violence against women and their unborn children...If abortion were to become illegal, I would not support punishment for women who abort...Most women seeking abortions state that they felt forced or coerced into their decision. I would not support a system that punishes those who are already victimized.[23]

---

[22] https://www.lifesitenews.com/news/pro-life-leaders-appalled-after-national-review-columnist-calls-for-hanging.
[23] https://www.lifesitenews.com/news/pro-life-leaders-appalled-after-national-review-columnist-calls-for-hanging.

Scott Mahurin director of Florida Preborn Rescue in December 2018:

> However, after I signed the petition [calling for the Florida House of Representative to criminalize abortion and make it a felony for anyone procuring or performing an abortion], I began to have second thoughts. After further reflection, and rereading it, I believe that there was a loophole in the petition that would leave women vulnerable to prosecution for having an abortion, which has never been done in the history of the United States, even when abortion was illegal...Abolish Human Abortion sponsoring total abortion bans is fine. But taking the next step to prosecuting women is not just immoral, but completely foolhardy given our current political situation.[24]

INDOCTRINATED

The secular Pro-Life movement argues that we should not consider women who murder their preborn children perpetrators in the crime because of the effectiveness of cultural indoctrination by the Pro-abortion movement. They say that for generations we have been lied to about life in the prenatal stages of development. In particular, women have been told that the fetus is only a clump of cells. The claim is that we have been inundated with junk science, misleading

---

[24] Scott Mahurin, *Bad Roots, Bad Fruits: A Pro-Life Challenge to AHA/Abolish Human Abortion* (self-published, 2018).

evidence, and powerful emotional appeals, which are designed to force feed the population all the necessary ingredients to believe that an image bearing preborn child is no more than non-viable excisable tissue. They insist that the propaganda promoted by this culture which loves death and hates God has been so successful that we need to treat abortive women as victims; the women have been too indoctrinated by these lies to know that they are killing their own children.[25]

Admittedly, there has been a massive effort on the part of our pro-abortion culture to manage the perception of the people. A substantial amount of resources, time, money, and education have been poured into inculcating the population with their agenda. Despite all the scientific advances in technology, biology, genetics, and embryology—all of which confirm what God has said in special revelation—we must be honest and say that pro-death marketing has been successful in controlling the conversation and manipulating the language of the discussion. The profound impact which

---

[25] As another example, consider this quote from Ben Shapiro. "The second reason is because I think that we in our society have unfortunately gotten to such a point that an entire generation has been indoctrinated to believe – particularly an entire generation of women, since that's what we're talking about here – has been indoctrinated to believe that a baby is a polyp and so when they remove it, I'm not sure there's the necessary mens rea, the criminal intent necessary for prosecution. The typical pro-life position here is that the woman is a victim of abortion nearly as much as the baby is. There is an entire abortion industry that is geared toward teaching women that babies are not babies and that getting a baby aborted is in fact a betterment of their life. So no, I am not in favor of prosecuting women for abortions. Ben Shapiro, Q&A, UC Berkley, 2017, https://www.youtube.com/watch?v=aP_9cRUzqMw&feature=youtu.be&t=1h38s.

decades of pro-abortion rhetoric and lies has had on our society cannot be questioned. What is in question is the impact this has had on the necessary intention or knowledge of wrongdoing which constitutes part of a crime in general, and on the Christian, who applies a biblical ethic in dealing with this issue in particular.

We will now expose the inconsistency and impotency of this line of argumentation. First, let's examine how indoctrinated the culture has become. Then we will take a closer look at the lack of equity with which the secular Pro-Life establishment seeks to apply this cultural indoctrination.

The light of nature has already fractured the pro-abortion lies concerning the clump of cells argument. The past 50 years have seen amazing growth in various biological disciplines along with technological advancements to make the needed observations. This has been so powerful that the pro-abortion lobby has had to concede the point. They have shifted the narrative, nuancing its arguments of personhood and arbitrary points as to when viable life begins, and thus when constitutional rights are granted by the state.[26] The secular Pro-Life establishment has fallen into this trap, among others, which we will discuss later. Changes in the narrative take time to filter down to the population and you will find that average people on the street still employ some version of the clump-

[26] This sentence is a jab at the current American milieu that the secular Pro-Life establishment is willing to join in as they bow to almighty SCOTUS. It is the opposite of what God has said, and of what the framers of our nation put to parchment in the declaration of independence. "We hold these truths to be self-evident, that all men are created equal, that they are endowed by their Creator with certain unalienable rights, that among these are Life, Liberty and the pursuit of Happiness."

of-cells argument. However, this is slowly passing away as the pro-abortion narrative changes its emphasis to which arbitrary stages of life should be given protection under the constitution. Interestingly, it is rarely heard at abortion mills from women that have scheduled appointments to kill their preborn children.

Has the pro-abortion disinformation machine indoctrinated our culture to such an extent that we lack the necessary intention or knowledge of wrongdoing which constitutes part of a crime (Mens Rea)? Our current laws do not reflect this. The Unborn Victims of Violence Act of 2004 recognizes an embryo or fetus in utero as a legal victim if they are injured or killed during the commission of any of over 60 listed federal crimes of violence. The law defines "child in utero" as "a member of the species *Homo sapiens*, at any stage of development, who is carried in the womb".[27] Thirty-eight (38) states currently recognize the "unborn child" (the term usually used) or fetus as a homicide victim, and twenty-three (23) of those states apply this principle throughout the period of pre-natal development.[28] This shows the failure of the pro-abortion culture to completely indoctrinate our society to the elimination of Mens Rea.

This leads to our next point, which is the inconsistent application of the secular Pro-Life indoctrination argument. This section will expose the cognitive dissonance of the secular Pro-Life establishment which seeks to cast the

---

[27] Text of the law can be found here: https://www.gpo.gov/fdsys/pkg/PLAW-108publ212/pdf/PLAW-108publ212.pdf.

[28] http://www.ncsl.org/research/health/fetal-homicide-state-laws.aspx.

abortive mother as victim rather than perpetrator. There will be variations from state to state, but the overall structure remains the same. We will take Texas as our example:

> Texas penal code Sec. 1.07. DEFINITIONS. (a) In this code: (26) "Individual" means a human being who is alive, including an unborn child at every stage of gestation from fertilization until birth.[29]
> TITLE 5. OFFENSES AGAINST THE PERSON, CHAPTER 19. CRIMINAL HOMICIDE
> Sec. 19.01. TYPES OF CRIMINAL HOMICIDE. (a) A person commits criminal homicide if he intentionally, knowingly, recklessly, or with criminal negligence causes the death of an individual.
> (b) Criminal homicide is murder, capital murder, manslaughter, or criminally negligent homicide.[30]

The remainder of chapter 19 of the penal code details the differences and requirements for the four categories of criminal homicide. Each of those categories and subcategories are determined by various degrees to which the Mens Rea is met. The type of intent and the level of knowledge is weighed into which form of criminal homicide the individual is charged with. Notice that in each case it is the death of an *Individual* as defined earlier to include unborn children at every stage of development. Chapter 19 of Criminal Homicide ends with prosecutorial exemptions that deal particularly with the homicide of unborn children.

---

[29] https://statutes.capitol.texas.gov/Docs/PE/htm/PE.1.htm#1.07.
[30] https://statutes.capitol.texas.gov/Docs/PE/htm/PE.19.htm.

> Sec. 19.06. APPLICABILITY TO CERTAIN CONDUCT. This chapter does not apply to the death of an unborn child if the conduct charged is:
> (1) conduct committed by the mother of the unborn child;
> (2) a lawful medical procedure performed by a physician or other licensed health care provider with the requisite consent, if the death of the unborn child was the intended result of the procedure;
> (3) a lawful medical procedure performed by a physician or other licensed health care provider with the requisite consent as part of an assisted reproduction as defined by Section 160.102, Family Code;[31]

In Texas, when the death of an unborn child meets the detailed requirements listed above, the perpetrator is charged with criminal homicide. As we said in the last section, this alone debunks the indoctrination argument. When we look at the exemptions listed in 19.6.1, first we see the mother that kills her *own* preborn child at any time up till birth is exempt from prosecution (Pro-Life second victim law). The abortionist and the IVF scientist that kill preborn children are also exempt from prosecution, so long as they commit the homicidal acts in accordance with the proper state regulations.

---

[31] This exemption deals with IVF and connected research, another form of slaughter of preborn image bearers that the church by and large ignores.

The aforementioned criminal homicide codes dealing with death of preborn children are all written by the secular Pro-Life establishment. They show an interesting phenomenon when it comes to their cultural indoctrination argument, which denies equal justice and considers the abortive mother as the second victim. According to them, there is only one particular class of people that have been completely indoctrinated by the propaganda of the culture of death: mothers who kill their own preborn children.

If a man kills a pregnant woman under these laws, he will be charged with two counts of homicide. If a woman kills a pregnant woman under these laws, she will be charged with two counts of homicide. If a pregnant woman kills another pregnant woman under these laws, she will be charged with two counts of homicide. It is only when a pregnant woman kills her own preborn child that she is exempt from homicide prosecution. *Every person in these examples has been indoctrinated by the same propaganda from our culture of death.* The Mens Rea has been met for the prosecution of criminal homicide in each case. The secular Pro-Life establishment, inconsistent with the laws they write and promote, asserts that the only indoctrinated class of people are women that kill their own preborn children.

As we look at the secular Pro-Life argument against providing equal justice, a great deal of irony begins to emerge. A strong case could be made that the secular Pro-life establishment is responsible for some of the most impactful indoctrination through the laws it writes, supports, and passes. Pro-Life leader/Activist and former abortion worker Abby Johnson has rightly said, "My goal is not simply to make abortion illegal. If that is our goal, it is shortsighted...My goal is to make abortion unthinkable..."[32] She and her ilk undercut the foundation of that philosophy by their uncompromising position against prosecutorial equal justice for women who murder their preborn children. The secular Pro-Life establishment perpetuates the indoctrination by not treating mothers like all other perpetrators of criminal homicide. By imposing victimhood on the perpetrator, they not only deny justice to the true victim, but expose the diminished value which they bestow upon the preborn image bearer. The secular Pro-Life establishment says it wants to make abortion unthinkable, but it utterly fails to do so by the laws it supports, which deny the only reason that makes abortion unthinkable, *imago dei.*

COERCED

Read Abby Johnson's quote at the beginning of this chapter again. She very clearly and succinctly outlines the next argument of the secular Pro-Life argument against applying equal justice. "Most women seeking abortions state that they felt forced or coerced into their decision. I would not support a system that punishes those who are already victimized." Johnson and those like her buttress their insistence that the abortive mother should be considered a second victim with the idea that she is forced or coerced to participate in the murder of her child.

Tragically, there *are* women who are victimized and forced to kill their preborn children. This is a tactic often employed

---

[32] https://ccdenver.org/abby-johnson-we-must-change-this-culture/.

in the sex trafficking industry. It is also a common practice when abusers hide evidence of incestuous child rape. It is a sickening reality that a woman can be victimized sexually and then victimized again in the murder of her preborn child, in order that she may then return to repeated sexual attacks. The horrific nature of these crimes cannot be understated nor overlooked. However, the reality is that these extreme cases make up a small number of the 3500+ daily abortions in our country.[33] It is true shame that we would minimize the atrocity they suffer by lowering the threshold of victimization to include women who willingly murder their preborn children.

When we ask for equal justice, we are not searching for new laws. Rather, we wish for laws already in place to be applied and enforced *equally*. Here is an example. Texas, like most states, spells out in its laws what constitutes coercion, force, or duress and how to apply those definitions in these cases.

> PENAL CODE
> TITLE 2. GENERAL PRINCIPLES OF CRIMINAL RESPONSIBILITY
> CHAPTER 8. GENERAL DEFENSES TO CRIMINAL RESPONSIBILITY
> Sec. 8.05. DURESS. (a) It is an affirmative defense to prosecution that the actor engaged in the proscribed

[33]The following links point to the reasons given for the abortion. https://www.cdc.gov/mmwr/volumes/66/ss/ss6624a1.htm?s_cid=ss6624a1_w.
http://www.johnstonsarchive.net/policy/abortion/abreasons.html#2.

> conduct because he was compelled to do so by threat of imminent death or serious bodily injury to himself or another.
> (b) In a prosecution for an offense that does not constitute a felony, it is an affirmative defense to prosecution that the actor engaged in the proscribed conduct because he was compelled to do so by force or threat of force.
> (c) Compulsion within the meaning of this section exists only if the force or threat of force would render a person of reasonable firmness incapable of resisting the pressure.
> (d) The defense provided by this section is unavailable if the actor intentionally, knowingly, or recklessly placed himself in a situation in which it was probable that he would be subjected to compulsion.
> (e) It is no defense that a person acted at the command or persuasion of his spouse, unless he acted under compulsion that would establish a defense under this section.[34]

We do not need to create a new class of victims for coercion. All we need to do is apply just laws equally to this form of homicide. Sec. 8.05.e eliminates nearly all the cases that are mentioned by the secular Pro-Life establishment in their coercion argument. The rest are protected by this section of law. Trafficked women aside, nearly every example

[34] https://statutes.capitol.texas.gov/Docs/PE/htm/PE.8.htm.

I have heard from the secular Pro-Life establishment is some variation of *their parents/boyfriend/husband will kick them out/leave them/not provide for them.* In these cases, there is a lot of pressure placed on them. This pressure, however, is by no means legal coercion. To help simplify the scenario, replace "aborting preborn child" with "killing one or two-year-old child." The defense is not valid. It treats image bearers arbitrarily. The problem is our sinful partiality, and it is exposed when we compare our thoughts of a one-year-old child with a preborn child. Are they not both image bearers? When we strip away all the unjust Pro-Life legislation (explained in the next chapter) we see that *our current laws are already equipped to deal with all of the secular Pro-Life establishments objections to applying equal justice to all forms of homicide.* The law is designed to offer due process to every individual case. Evidence is collected and the District Attorney decides, based off the evidence, if the prosecutorial procedures will begin. He decides what charges to make (if any) from the evidence that determines the level of intent and knowledge. A jury is presented with all of the evidence, including that of the defense. Protections for the defendant are intentionally placed throughout the entire process. Again, our current system of law, in respect to criminal homicide, is capable of answering judiciously all of the secular Pro-Life establishment's stated concerns. All they are left with is an emotional plea, one that, while it is illogical, remains very powerful to those they have continued to indoctrinate.

The secular Pro-Life establishment has been successful in killing abolitionist bills that seek equal justice by removing all the Pro-Life exemptions and legislation. They spin the phrasing of their opposition (those seeking prosecution of all principle actors and accomplices in criminal homicide) by saying things like this: This bill targets women, or makes women vulnerable to death penalty, or seeks to execute women, or some similar inflammatory, emotionally charged headline. These accusations are misleading at best. Unfortunately, we are forced to have our conversations in terms of how to treat the woman that kills her preborn child, because the secular Pro-Life movement has continued to perpetuate the abortive mother as the only class of people that should be exempt from prosecution in any form of criminal homicide. The truth is that they are targeting women. We are saying that Texas rightly calls abortion criminal homicide, though it is the only form of criminal homicide that is not adjudicated as such. We want the Pro-Life exemptions removed and to have abortion treated like all other forms of criminal homicide, where all of the principle actors and accomplices enter into the judicial process. That is equal justice.

PROXIMATE JUSTICE/LACK OF EFFECTIVENESS

Why do the states target abortionists and treat women as their victims? Clarke D. Forsythe says:

> This idea is based on three policy judgments: the point of abortion law is effective enforcement against abortionists, the woman is the second victim of the abortionist, and

prosecuting women is counterproductive to the goal of effective enforcement of the law against abortionists.[35]

As was laid out in chapter 1, the image of God on fallen man has been corrupted. The resulting noetic effects of the fall make it impossible for us to judge properly according to that image. All people have an internal longing for justice, but because of our sin we are incapable of executing it with the perfect precision demanded by our Creator. This will continue to the end of to the age, when the groaning of creation is silenced, and all things made new. Yet in this life we are to move toward what Steven Garber, author and director of The Washington Institute, calls *proximate justice* even as we await the perfection of the new heavens and new earth. In his often-sourced article he says, "Proximate justice realizes that something is better than nothing. It allows us to make peace with some justice, some mercy, all the while realizing that it will only be in the new heaven and new earth that we find all our longings finally fulfilled, that we will see all of God's demands finally met. It is only then and there we will see all of the conditions for human flourishing finally in place, socially, economically, and politically."[36]

This concept lays the foundation of the secular Pro-Life establishment's argument against pursuing equal justice for the murder of preborn children. It places this true concept in a falsely pragmatic line of thinking which says we will take

---

[35] http://www.aul.org/law-articles/why-the-states-did-not-prosecute-women-for-abortion-before-roe-v-wade/.

[36] http://www.washingtoninst.org/wp-content/uploads/2009/03/Proximate_Justice_Comment.pdf.

what little justice that we can get. The secular Pro-Life establishment argument goes like this: We should not prosecute women who murder their own preborn children because it would make it more difficult to prosecute the abortionist, and it is the abortionist that is the primary problem. To be fair to the secular Pro-Life establishment, this has been the position of our nation and it has always failed to provide equal justice in the murder of preborn children. We see in the *Roe v. Wade* transcripts and in the decision that this inconsistency played a large part in the unjust ruling.[37] Our historical failure to apply equal justice for the fetus, with the parents as primary actors in the crime, is proof that we do not believe the fetus to be a human child with equal rights endowed by the Creator. Our duty is to repent and obey the commands of God, irrespective of the precedent and longevity of a previous failure to do so.

---

[37] [*Roe v. Wade* decision Footnote 54] When Texas urges that a fetus is entitled to Fourteenth Amendment protection as a person, it faces a dilemma. Neither in Texas nor in any other State are all abortions prohibited. Despite broad proscription, an exception always exists. The exception contained [410 U.S. 113, 158] in Art. 1196 for an abortion procured or attempted by medical advice for the purpose of saving the life of the mother is typical. But if the fetus is a person who is not to be deprived of life without due process of law, and if the mother's condition is the sole determinant, does not the Texas exception appear to be out of line with the amendment's command?

There are other inconsistencies between Fourteenth Amendment status and the typical abortion statute. It has already been pointed out, n. 49, supra, that in Texas the woman is not a principal or an accomplice with respect to an abortion upon her. If the fetus is a person, why is the woman not a principal or an accomplice? Further, the penalty for criminal abortion specified by Art. 1195 is significantly less than the maximum penalty for murder prescribed by Art. 1257 of the Texas Penal Code. If the fetus is a person, may the penalties be different?

It is historically true that including the mother as an accomplice to the crime makes it more difficult to prosecute the abortionist, making this a bedrock to the secular Pro-Life argument for treating the abortive mother as a victim. The following is from the Texas code of criminal procedure. The language has not changed since this 1857 article:

> TITLE 1. CODE OF CRIMINAL PROCEDURE
> CHAPTER 38. EVIDENCE IN CRIMINAL ACTIONS
> Art. 38.14. TESTIMONY OF ACCOMPLICE. A conviction cannot be had upon the testimony of an accomplice unless corroborated by other evidence tending to connect the defendant with the offense committed; and the corroboration is not sufficient if it merely shows the commission of the offense.[38]

The argument is that, by treating the abortive woman as an accomplice to the crime, her testimony against the abortionist, *if uncorroborated*, is not sufficient to bring a conviction against the abortionist to pass. Therefore, in order to successfully convict the abortionist, we must consider the abortive mother as the second victim of the crime. For the first 200+ years of our nation, the application of this common law and article from the code of criminal procedure covering the testimony of accomplice made it virtually impossible to convict an abortionist because of the lack of corroborating evidence. This had a huge impact on the unconstitutional

---

[38] https://statutes.capitol.texas.gov/Docs/CR/htm/CR.38.htm.

ruling of the Supreme Court *Roe v. Wade* decision, which we will further detail in a later chapter. Decades of growth in our understanding and application in medical science and technology has bridged that gap, and now we can produce the necessary corroborating evidence apart from extra witnesses. While there is some added difficulty when we seek to prosecute all parties involved in the murder of preborn children, it is by no means insurmountable and should not deter us from seeking to apply justice equally.

The second premise is that the primary problem in abortion lies with the abortionist. By focusing on the abortionist, we will eliminate the problem of abortion because they happen to be the root cause. The thought is that it is the abortionist and the aforementioned indoctrination which is creating the demand. Proximate justice and the lack of effectiveness in prosecuting the abortionist demands that we continue our historic attack against the abortionist alone. As Clarke D. Forsythe, AUL Senior Counsel, says, "the goal is effective enforcement of the law against abortionists."

If you go back to the top of this chapter and reread the secular Pro-Life leaders' quotations, you will see a pattern emerge: compassion for the woman and justice for the abortionist. This false dichotomy is so entrenched in the ideology that it has become the emotional driving force of this argument. To help enshrine this, even Christian apologists like Denny Burk and Scott Klusendorf add a moral and legal culpability separation. In an article from March of 2016, Denny Burk says, "Pro-lifers believe that it should be illegal to perform abortions. Thus we favor policies that punish those who perform abortions, not the mothers who allow them.

Why? The answer has both a moral and legal dimension."[39] The lion's share of the article details this separation.

The secular Pro-Life establishment seeks to use this separation of moral and legal culpability to harmonize the irreconcilable inconsistencies of their second victim argument. Christian apologists in the secular Pro-Life establishment are forced to maintain a moral/legal distinction because of the gospel message of Christ, our risen Lord, crucified for sinners. Victims are not guilty by virtue of their victimhood. Only the guilty are in need of forgiveness, and therefore in need of the Redeemer.

He ends his article by saying, "And it also clarifies that the pro-life movement has never sought to punish women by force of law for getting an abortion. Rather, the focus has been on treating them with care and compassion. Anyone unaware of this history does not understand the pro-life position." Notice that care and compassion belong to the abortive mother and punishment belongs to the abortionist.

This is a false dichotomy, and a misunderstanding of compassion. Both the abortive mother and the abortionist deserve justice, and both are in need of compassion. Everyone that participates in the killing of preborn children deserves to be delivered up to God's minister, for he bears the sword of retributive justice. As Christians, we should strive more than all to offer earnest assistance to each of the parties involved, working with their physical circumstances and addressing whatever factors are, in their minds, pushing them to seek to

---

[39] http://www.dennyburk.com/trying-to-clean-up-after-donald-trumps-abortion-mess/.

kill these children. Christians should have the most compassion and concern for the physical and spiritual condition of all of the actors involved. We must offer them the hope we have in Christ, the provider of both physical and spiritual needs. We should remember that the killing of these preborn children is primarily an attack against God, and that God's just condemnation abides on all of those involved.[40] But God is full of steadfast love and forgives all types of transgressions, iniquity, and sins, even those of the abortionist, the abortive parents, and all who facilitate the murder. Their sin has no power over the victory of our Lord. His mediatorial work is for all who come to Him.

WHAT HAS GOD SAID ABOUT EQUAL JUSTICE?

The mouth of the fool has been silenced by his weak and faulty reasoning being exposed and refuted. Christians have long confessed that the holy Scripture is the only sufficient, certain, and infallible rule of all saving knowledge, faith, and obedience. This means that there is no part of our lives to which God has not directly spoken. We, as Christians, are given special revelation, the very mind of Christ as priests in His kingdom, and we are to apply this Christian ethic in our daily lives as we image our Lord in time and space. This section will consider what God has said about how we are to apply justice.

I want to remind the discerning reader that the purview of this chapter is our treatment of an abortive mother when

---

[40] I would like to draw your attention again to footnote 5 in the first chapter.

abortion is criminalized. I would argue that the entirety of my presentation in this chapter ought to be applied to everyone that participates in the unjust killing, not just the woman that procures the abortion. This would include anyone that helps in the facilitation of the crime as principle actors, accomplices, or co-conspirators.[41] Equal justice as it pertains to abortion in particular assumes a few things that will not be addressed in this chapter (although subsequent chapters will address some of them). First, the value of human life is solely contingent on the image of God that they are created in. Second, abortion is the unjust taking of human life from the point of conception. Third, the civil government is the minister of God that bears the sword of justice.

There is not explicit direction in Scripture on how to treat those who procure, facilitate, or perform abortions. There are, however, explicit teachings and examples in Mosaic case law from which we can by general equity glean how to differentiate forms of homicide. There are also principals of responsibility in the text.[42] Though proximate justice is all we have due to sin and its effects, our nation, as previously shown, applies natural law fairly well.[43] But this is not our purpose in the present chapter. We are going to address ourselves to the impartial and equal application of justice in the homicide laws that already exist.

---

[41] The reason that I am focusing on the abortive woman in this chapter is to directly refute the prolife assertion that abortive women are victims in this crime.

[42] All the Texas laws mentioned in this chapter are examples of this and attest to the use of general equity and natural law.

[43] We are not asking for new laws or regulations. We are asking that current laws pertaining to homicide be applied equally to all people.

Scripture is full of commands and wisdom about justice and its application. It speaks of weights and measures, just balances, even scales, and partiality. These biblical themes are common to both believer and unbeliever and are deeply entrenched in the psyche of our judicial landscape. We will look at a small selection of these verses presently. They will show not only what God expects from His creatures, but how prolific the theme of equal justice is in His word.

> Better is a little with righteousness than great income with injustice. The mind of a man plans his way, But the Lord directs his steps. A divine decision is in the lips of the king; His mouth should not err in judgment. A just balance and scales belong to the Lord; All the weights of the bag are His concern. It is an abomination for kings to commit wicked acts, For a throne is established on righteousness. (Proverbs 16:8-12).

God's appointed servant bears the sword of justice as His representative, applying equal justice with a just balance and scales that belong to God Himself (verses 10-12). To show unwarranted partiality in applying justice is evil and an abomination in the eyes of God. Thus, it is an act of wickedness before God to pervert justice by showing deference to a special class of people that commit homicide[44]

[44] Leviticus 19:15 says, "You shall do no injustice in judgment; you shall not be partial to the poor nor defer to the great, but you are to judge your neighbor fairly." By stating the extreme ends, this verse in particular commands us to apply justice equally irrespective of the category of people that we are, but solely on the evidence in the case.

(namely, mothers who kill their own preborn children). Here are more examples from Proverbs which speak of equal justice:

> He who justifies the wicked and he who condemns the righteous, both of them alike are an abomination to the Lord. (Proverbs 17:15).

> To show partiality to the wicked is not good, *Nor* to thrust aside the righteous in judgment. (Proverbs 18:5).

> Differing weights and differing measures, both of them are abominable to the Lord. (Proverbs 20:10).

> A false balance is an abomination to the Lord, but a just weight is His delight. When pride comes, then comes dishonour, but with the humble is wisdom. The integrity of the upright will guide them, but the crookedness of the treacherous will destroy them. (Proverbs 11:1-3).

> These also are sayings of the wise. To show partiality in judgment is not good. He who says to the wicked, "You are righteous," Peoples will curse him, nations will abhor him; But to those who rebuke the *wicked* will be delight, And a good blessing will come upon them. He kisses the lips who gives a right answer. (Proverbs 24:23-26).

This small sample shows us what God thinks about justice, His delight in its impartial application, and the wickedness He finds in its corruption. The idea of applying equal weights and measures/a just balance/even scales/equal justice is not limited to the general principles of wisdom spoken to us in the Proverbs. When He constituted the nation of Israel, God had quite a bit to say about these things. We are not the physical seed of Abraham, the ethnic nation of Israel; the positive laws[45] imposed on them do not apply to us in exactly

[45] This is from a very good article "THE CONSEQUENCES OF POSITIVE LAW: The Particular Baptists' Use of Inferential Reasoning in Theology," Samuel Renihan, JIRBS (2016): 125-126. To define positive law, we must first define moral law. Moral law refers to the universal law of nature as expressed in the Decalogue, binding on all mankind at all times. Positive laws are specific laws given by God for a specific people and for a specific time. For example, that Adam should not eat of the tree of the knowledge of good and evil was a positive law. Apart from a direct divine command, it was not morally wrong for Adam to eat of that tree. But God positively prohibited Adam from eating it. Since Adam had a moral obligation to obey God, eating from the tree became sinful. Similarly, circumcision, Passover, the sacrificial system, baptism, and the Lord's Supper are all positive ordinances. They are built on commands that must be obeyed, strictly and exactly. The observance of these ordinances was not the result of some inherent morality in such practices, but simply obedience to the God who issued the commands. Therefore, failure to obey these commands was disobedience to God and just as sinful as an inherently immoral act. Adam fell because of a violation of a positive command. Nadab and Abihu were consumed for violation of positive laws. Positive laws were no less binding, but they were of a different character than the moral law. Positive laws are given in the context of covenantal life and worship. Thus they rise and fall with their covenants. New Testament believers are not required to follow the positive laws of Israel beyond their general equity (2LCF 19.4). We are free to eat bacon with a clear conscience because it is perfectly moral to do so. Under the Old Covenant, it was forbidden by positive law.

the same way. They are, however of use to us in their general equity,[46] which we see expressed in natural law. Here are a few helpful examples.

> Then I charged your judges at that time, saying, 'Hear *the cases* between your fellow countrymen, and judge righteously between a man and his fellow countryman, or the alien who is with him. You shall not show partiality in judgment; you shall hear the small and the great alike. You shall not fear man, for the judgment is God's. The case that is too hard for you, you shall bring to me, and I will hear it.' I commanded you at that time all the things that you should do. (Deuteronomy 1:16-18a).

> You shall appoint for yourself judges and officers in all your towns which the Lord your God is giving you, according to your tribes, and they shall judge the people with righteous judgment. You shall not distort justice; you shall not be partial, and you shall not take a bribe, for a bribe blinds the eyes of the wise and perverts the words of the righteous. Justice, *and only* justice, you shall pursue, that you may live and possess the land which the Lord your God is giving you. (Deuteronomy 16:18-20)

Another good article on the distinction between moral law and positive law is "Baptism, a positive inflexible Law" Sidney Dyer JIRBS (2017): 71.

[46] The following article on general equity and positive law is helpful. http://reformedlibertarian.com/articles/theology/1-cor-513-is-the-general-equity-of-deut-2221/.

> You shall not have in your bag differing weights, a large and a small. You shall not have in your house differing measures, a large and a small. You shall have a full and just weight; you shall have a full and just measure, that your days may be prolonged in the land which the Lord your God gives you. For everyone who does these things, everyone who acts unjustly is an abomination to the Lord your God. (Deuteronomy 25:13-16).

We can draw clear concepts from the imposed laws, regulations, and commands of God to His earthly people, such as ideas of righteous judgment, partiality in judgment, fear of man, distortion of justice, benefits of equal justice, and sanctions for partiality. In other passages, God rebukes His deacons of justice for their unjust judgments, calling for repentance. We should take these indictments most seriously.

> God takes His stand in His own congregation; He judges in the midst of the rulers. How long will you judge unjustly and show partiality to the wicked? *Selah.* Vindicate the weak and fatherless; Do justice to the afflicted and destitute. Rescue the weak and needy; deliver *them* out of the hand of the wicked. They do not know nor do they understand; they walk about in darkness; all the foundations of the earth are shaken. Isaid, "You are gods, and all of you are sons of the Most High. "Nevertheless you will die like men and fall like *any* one of the princes." Arise, O God,

judge the earth! For it is You who possesses all the nations. (Psalm 82).

'Thus says the Lord God, "Enough, you princes of Israel; put away violence and destruction, and practice justice and righteousness. Stop your expropriations from My people," declares the Lord God. "You shall have just balances, a just ephah and a just bath. (Ezekiel 45:9-10).

He has told you, O man, what is good; And what does the Lord require of you But to do justice, to love kindness, And to walk humbly with your God? The voice of the Lord will call to the city—And it is sound wisdom to fear Your name: "Hear, O tribe. Who has appointed its time? "Is there yet a man in the wicked house, *Along with* treasures of wickedness And a short measure *that is* cursed? "Can I justify wicked scales And a bag of deceptive weights? "For the rich men of *the* city are full of violence, Her residents speak lies, And their tongue is deceitful in their mouth. "So also I will make *you* sick, striking you down, Desolating *you* because of your sins. "You will eat, but you will not be satisfied, And your vileness will be in your midst. You will *try to* remove *for safekeeping*, But you will not preserve *anything*, And what you do preserve I will give to the sword. "You will sow but you will not reap. You will tread the olive but will not anoint yourself

> with oil; And the grapes, but you will not drink wine. (Micah 6:8-15).

> If, however, you are fulfilling the royal law according to the Scripture, "You shall love your neighbor as yourself," you are doing well. But if you show partiality, you are committing sin *and* are convicted by the law as transgressors. For whoever keeps the whole law and yet stumbles in one *point*, he has become guilty of all. (James 2:8-10)

CONCLUSION

Scott Mahurin, a professing Christian and director of Florida Preborn Rescue says this, "Abolish Human Abortion sponsoring total abortion bans is fine. But taking the next step to prosecuting women is not *just immoral*, but completely foolhardy given our current political situation."[47]

To say something is immoral is to say something is sin. Mahurin's statement, strong as it is, must be taken seriously and examined. He claims that it is immoral to prosecute women for the crime of unjustly killing their preborn child with premeditation. In other words, it is sinful to apply equal justice to this form of homicide, which is quite the opposite of what God has said about justice. He is advocating for

---

[47] "Bad Roots, Bad Fruits" Scott Mahurin (2018).

partiality in justice which God calls an abomination. Ironically, what he is promoting is immoral. It is sinful.[48]

When you read the secular Pro-Life position stating that women who kill their own preborn children should be the only perpetrators of any type of homicide who are excluded from prosecution, do you hear the voice of the serpent whispering in your ear, "Did God really say to apply equal justice? ... Did God really say that partiality or deference is injustice in judgment? ... Did God really say that false balances are an abomination to Him?"

Redeemed in Christ, you have been given His mind and are being transformed into His image. By the work of the gospel in your life, you can stand with Him on His word and say as He did, "Thus says the Lord". The Secular Pro-Life position is not the Christian position when it comes to the equal application of justice in the murder of the preborn. At all costs, at all times, in all places, we are commanded to say with confidence, "Thus says the Lord."

In a 2016 townhall, Donald Trump said that abortive women should be prosecuted. Scott Klusendorf, a professing Christian and president of Life Training Institute wrote this in a response, "But again, even if pro-lifers are inconsistent on the issue of consequences, how would that in anyway prove the unborn are not human or that intentionally killing them

---

[48] I debated this topic with Scott Mahurin in May of 2019. He also used the words unjust, unbiblical, and immoral to describe the position of equal justice. When directly asked if it was sinful, he backed off and said no, but that it was an error. In his closing statement he kicked the rhetoric up a notch and claimed that those who hold this position do not know the gospel and are lost.

is justified? At best, it proves individual pro-lifers are failing to consistently apply their ethic."

The secular Pro-Life establishment is inconsistent on the issue of consequences. These inconsistencies, in the issue of consequences, had a large impact on the unjust *Roe v. Wade* ruling. Footnote 17 from this chapter demonstrates that the justices in 1973 argued and made their decision in the way Klusendorf denies possible. The justices reason that the lack of consistent consequences does prove that the unborn are not human and that intentionally killing them is justified.

"Failing to consistently apply their ethic" is a euphemism for sin. Sin is any want of conformity to, or transgression of, the law of God.[49] As priests in the kingdom of God we are required to consistently apply a Christian ethic, the word of God, to all our dealings in this world. This includes how we seek justice, apply justice, and fight injustice. God calls it sin when we are not faithful to apply our Christian ethic consistently, and He calls us to repent. May God grant us repentance and conform us more to the image of His Son through the truth of His word. We must lay down this sinful secular Pro-Life doctrine which denies the application of equal justice and with Christ say, "Thus says the Lord."

---

[49] Westminster Catechism, question fourteen.

Iniquitous Decrees & Calling Evil Good

The second uncompromising pillar of the secular Pro-Life establishment is its long-term legal strategy to stop the killing of unborn children through abortion. It is their intention to regulate abortion to the fullest extent by, and in a manner consistent with, the decisions of the Supreme Court of the United States (SCOTUS). When the *Roe v. Wade* decision can finally be reversed, by the changing of the political climate and makeup of the court, only then can regulations be increased until abortion is finally made illegal.[50] For decades the secular Pro-Life movement has insisted on laws that regulate abortion to the fullest extent by, and in a manner consistent with the decisions of SCOTUS.[51]

We will examine this long-term strategy in two parts so I can give it the proximate justice that it is due. First, we will look at the law of the land and the myth of judicial supremacy, and then, the iniquitous decrees which codify that myth. We will finish the chapter, as is our custom, with a look at what God has said about this.

---

[50] In the next chapter we will deal with the secular Pro-Life strategy to eventually reverse the *Roe v. Wade* decision.
[51] This is the wording used in many of the individual state's official documents in regard to abortion legislation.

LAW OF THE LAND AND THE MYTH OF JUDICIAL SUPREMACY

National Right to Life states this in their overview of federal policy and abortion:

> In the United States, the basic legal framework governing the legality of abortion and the legal status of unborn human beings has been "federalized" primarily by decisions of the United States Supreme Court, rather than by acts of Congress.[52]

In defending their opposition to Texas HB896 abolishing abortion act, Texas Alliance for Life says this:

> Bans abortions on non-viable babies, which the Supreme Court does not permit. Requires the Texas Attorney General to ignore the Supreme Court, which is not possible. Criminalizes abortion for women on whom an abortion is performed. Women were never prosecuted for receiving an abortion in Texas beginning with the original law protecting unborn babies from abortion passed in 1854.[53]

To help us understand the secular Pro-Life establishment's capitulation to SCOTUS's demands on acceptable parameters to laws that regulate the killing of unborn

---

[52] National Right to Life State of Abortion, 2018, 30. https://www.nrlc.org/uploads/communications/stateofabortion2018.pdf.
[53] https://www.texasallianceforlife.org/2019-texas-legislature/.

children, we will start with a brief review of history and civics. These things will play an important role in this chapter and the next, so do bear with me. You will often hear the phrase, "the right to abortion or *Roe v. Wade* is the law of the land." This will come from all levels of each of the three branches of government, as well as from the vast majority of the people of this United States of America. It drives the pro-choice lobby as well as the Pro-Life establishment and their constituents. What is meant by the term *law of the land* and where does it come from? It means the established law of a nation or region.[54] In our nation, we the sovereign people have ordained the Constitution (and the laws made consistent with it) as the law of the land in order to establish justice.[55]

> ...This Constitution, and the laws of the United States which shall be made in pursuance thereof; and all treaties made, or which shall be made, under the authority of the United States, shall be the supreme law of the land; and the judges in every state shall be bound thereby, anything in the Constitution or laws of any State to the contrary notwithstanding...[56]

---

[54] *Merriam-Webster's Dictionary of Law* (Merriam-Webster 1996), 282.

[55] Preamble to the Constitution of the United States of America: We the People of the United States, in Order to form a more perfect Union, establish Justice, insure domestic Tranquility, provide for the common defense, promote the general Welfare, and secure the Blessings of Liberty to ourselves and our Posterity, do ordain and establish this Constitution for the United States of America.

[56] Article VI of the Constitution of the United States of America.

It is the consent of the governed which has established the law of the land through the Constitution. The question then becomes, "Where do laws consistent with the Constitution come from?" The people have delegated all authority to make laws in accordance with the Constitution to the legislature.[57] The judiciary has no authority to make laws. It is, however, given power to adjudicate the application of laws made by the legislature.[58] The decisions of the court are not law but rather rulings on a particular instantiation of the application of law. Let's start by looking at how some of the framers of the Constitution viewed the courts, their authority, and their relationship to the Constitution.

> Nothing in the Constitution has given them [the federal judges] a right to decide for the Executive, more than to the Executive to decide for them...The opinion which gives to the judges the right to decide what laws are constitutional and what not, not only

---

[57] **Article I** (Article 1 - Legislative) **Section 1:** All legislative Powers herein granted shall be vested in a Congress of the United States, which shall consist of a Senate and House of Representatives.

[58] **Article III** (Article 3 - Judicial) **Section 2** 1: The judicial Power shall extend to all Cases, in Law and Equity, arising under this Constitution, the Laws of the United States, and Treaties made, or which shall be made, under their Authority;—to all Cases affecting Ambassadors, other public Ministers and Consuls;—to all Cases of admiralty and maritime Jurisdiction;—to Controversies to which the United States shall be a Party;—to Controversies between two or more States;—between a State and Citizens of another State; —between Citizens of different States, —between Citizens of the same State claiming Lands under Grants of different States, and between a State, or the Citizens thereof, and foreign States, Citizens or Subjects.

for themselves, in their own sphere of action, but for the Legislature and Executive also in their spheres, would make the Judiciary a despotic branch. (Letter Thomas Jefferson to Abigail Adams, September 11, 1804).[59]

You seem...to consider the judges as the ultimate arbiters of all constitutional questions; a very dangerous doctrine indeed, and one which would place us under the despotism of an oligarchy. Our judges are as honest as other men, and not more so...and their power [is] the more dangerous, as they are in office for life and not responsible, as the other functionaries are, to the elective control. The Constitution has erected no such single tribunal, knowing that to whatever hands confided, with corruptions of time and party, its members would become despots. (Letter Thomas Jefferson to William Jarvis, Sept. 28, 1820).[60]

The judiciary of the United States is the subtle corps of sappers and miners constantly working under ground to undermine the foundations of our confederated fabric. They are construing our constitution from a co-ordination of a general and special government to a general and supreme one

[59] https://founders.archives.gov/documents/Jefferson/99-01-02-0348.
[60] https://founders.archives.gov/documents/Jefferson/98-01-02-1540.

alone. (Letter Thomas Jefferson to Thomas Ritchie, Dec. 25, 1820).[61]

One single object... [will merit] the endless gratitude of the society: that of restraining the judges from usurping legislation. (Letter to Edward Livingston, March 25, 1825).[62]

At the establishment of our constitutions, the judiciary bodies were supposed to be the most helpless and harmless members of the government. Experience, however, soon showed in what way they were to become the most dangerous; that the insufficiency of the means provided for their removal gave them a freehold and irresponsibility in office; that their decisions, seeming to concern individual suitors only, pass silent and unheeded by the public at large; that these decisions, nevertheless, become law by precedent, sapping, by little and little, the foundations of the constitution, and working its change by construction, before any one has perceived that that invisible and helpless worm has been busily employed in consuming its substance. In truth, man is not made to be trusted for life if secured against all liability to account. (Letter Thomas Jefferson to A. Coray, October 31, 1823).[63]

---

[61] https://founders.archives.gov/documents/Jefferson/98-01-02-1702.
[62] https://rotunda.upress.virginia.edu/founders/default.xqy?keys=FOEA-print-04-02-02-5077.
[63] https://rotunda.upress.virginia.edu/founders/default.xqy?keys=FOEA-print-04-02-02-3837.

> The judiciary, from the nature of its functions, will always be the least dangerous to the political rights of the Constitution; because it will be least in the capacity to annoy or injure them. (Alexander Hamilton Federalist 78).[64]

From its inception, we were warned about the Supreme Court's potential usurping of power. Through the history of our country we see this stream of judicial review, judicial supremacy, and legislating through the courts. The other branches, seeking to further their policies at one time or another, empowered this beast. Many point to *Marbury v. Madison* to justify judicial review and the previously quoted Article 6 of the Constitution (now called the supremacy clause). There is no indication in the Marshall court decision, nor in any of his subsequent writings, that the intent of this case was to establish the court as the final interpreter of the constitution.

The second half of the nineteenth century saw further accumulation of authority from the other branches as they sought to use the court to further their political agendas. In *Cooper v. Aaron* the court explicitly articulated the doctrine of judicial supremacy.

Article VI of the Constitution makes the Constitution the "supreme Law of the Land." In 1803, Chief Justice Marshall, speaking for a unanimous Court, referring to the Constitution as "the fundamental and paramount law of the

---

[64] Alexander Hamilton, James Madison, and John Jay, *The Federalist Papers* (Mineola, NY: Dover Publications, Inc., 2014)., 379.

nation," declared in the notable case of Marbury v. Madison, 1 Cranch 137, 177, that, "It is emphatically the province and duty of the judicial department to say what the law is." This decision declared the basic principle that the federal judiciary is supreme in the exposition of the law of the Constitution, and that principle has ever since been respected by this Court and the Country as a permanent and indispensable feature of our constitutional system. It follows that the interpretation of the Fourteenth Amendment enunciated by this Court in the Brown case is the supreme law of the land, and Art. VI of the Constitution makes it of binding effect on the States "any thing in the Constitution or Laws of any States to the Contrary notwithstanding." Every state legislator and executive and judicial officer is solemnly committed by oath taken pursuant to Art. VI, cl. 3, "to support this Constitution."...[65]

There has been no real political challenge to the Court's growing power grab for nearly a century. Instead, we have learned to bow to this oligarchy which lords itself over the constitution. We cannot continue to appease the tyrant, which only fuels it. We must confront it. We must put the constitutional chain back on that beast.

INIQUITOUS DECREES

Now that we have seen some of the reasons the secular Pro-Life establishment has obligated themselves to SCOTUS and the constructing of laws which regulate abortion in a manner

---

[65] SCOTUS opinion cooper v. aaron 358 u.s. 1 (1958) text of opinion can be found here **https://supreme.justia.com/cases/federal/us/358/1/**.

consistent with their decisions, let us consider some of these laws. Regulating abortion gives more than tacit permission; it definitionally governs, directs, and controls the killing of preborn children through rule and law. Rather than engendering an attitude of abhorrence for this slaughter, regulations legitimize the practice by dictating where, when, and how it is acceptable. Any law that sanctions the unjust killing of a human is by nature unjust. The regulatory laws that govern the killing of preborn children vary from state to state, though much of the language, parameters, and intent are similar. I will continue to use Texas as a model and speak generically.[66]

One of the greatest claimed victories for the secular Pro-Life establishment is the so-called "20-week ban," also titled the Pain Capable Act or Preborn Pain Act. This legislation states in (Texas) subchapter C 171.44, "Abortion of unborn child of 20 or more weeks post-fertilization age prohibited," and goes on to define terms and state exemptions. The secular Pro-Life establishment celebrates this legislative move, knowing that only *1.3% of abortions* take place in the 20+ post-fertilization time frame.[67] Even by humanistic standards of efficiency, to call these numbers a victory is appalling. This

---

[66] Health and Safety Code Title 2. Health Subtitle H. Public Health Provisions Chapter 171 Abortion,
https://statutes.capitol.texas.gov/Docs/HS/htm/HS.171.htm.

[67] According to the CDC abortion surveillance, 67% of abortions are performed before the 8-week post-fertilization time (this number is on a trajectory of exponential increase with the rise and proliferation of medical abortion pill). Extend that time frame by a few weeks, and 91% of abortions are performed before the 13-week post-fertilization mark. A staggering 98.7% of abortions are performed before the 20-week post-fertilization period. See www.cdc.gov/mmwr/volumes/66/ss/ss6624a1.htm.

act is called good and declared a successful Pro-Life law because, as they argue, it prohibits the killing of preborn children after they can feel pain or after the 20-week post-fertilization mark.[68] What the law does in the process is sanction, legitimize, and legalize the killing of younger preborn children (98.7%!). This law regulating the homicide of preborn children at this arbitrary stage of development says it is unacceptable to kill children that feel pain or are older than 20 weeks, but acceptable to kill those who do not. Now, no one in the Pro-Life industry will *say* that it is acceptable to kill preborn children younger than 20 weeks post-fertilization or that it is acceptable to kill preborn children that do not feel pain. Yet, that is exactly what this legislation intimates, as it regulates (governs, directs, and controls) the killing of these children based on their age and ability to feel pain.

The secular Pro-Life establishment seeks to make abortion unthinkable, but undermines that agenda by acting inconsistently with that idea. The pain capable/20-week ban is an act of injustice. In their zeal to prevent the killing of *some* preborn children, they unintentionally dehumanize all others. In essence, the ban denies that the worth of all human life is found solely in the image of God; or, as stated in our country's founding documents, "We hold these truths to be self-evident, that all men are created equal, that they are endowed by their Creator with certain unalienable Rights, that among these are

---

[68] Chapter 5 will further detail the difference in objectives of the secular Pro-Life establishment that focuses solely on the carnal result of saving as many babies as possible by any means, as opposed to the Christian objective of obedience in all circumstances and trusting in the God of Providence.

Life, Liberty, and the pursuit of Happiness."[69] It assigns worth by the arbitrary circumstance of ability to feel pain or age, discriminates, and determines the acceptability of killing that preborn child. This law devalues the worth of the younger child that does not feel pain and it denies justice for 98.7% of the victims of abortive homicide. A much stricter version of this kind of legislation would be the heart beat bill that relies on the same extrapolated principles and sets the arbitrary line of discrimination at the estimated time of a beating heart. This does prevent the killing of some children with the same unintended result. It also dehumanizes preborn humans that do not have a beating heart.[70]

Killing a 20-week or older post-fertilization child is horrific and evil, but is wrong for the same reason killing a 20-week or younger child is wrong. Killing a child that feels pain is inhumane and barbaric, but so is killing a child that does not feel pain, and for the same reason. Killing a child that has a heartbeat should be made illegal for the same reason that killing a child without a heartbeat should be criminalized. The reason is that children are created in the image of God and have their worth because of that image. Any deviation from this founding principle of justice will fail to make abortion unthinkable.

Another series of Pro-Life victories deal with the method in which the unborn child is killed or the tools used. These

---

[69] The Declaration of Independence.

[70] Sarah Cleveland a sonographer of 15 years has posted several articles on the effectiveness of heartbeat bills and testified at several legislative hearings on the topic. She has also written about ectopic pregnancy and late term abortion. https://soundtruthblog.wordpress.com.

popular laws address things such as partial birth abortion[71] and dismemberment abortions.[72] It is argued that certain methods of killing preborn children should be banned for the reasons stated in the partial birth act of 2003, "The Congress finds and declares the following: (1) A moral, medical, and ethical consensus exists that the practice of performing a partial-birth abortion is a gruesome and inhumane procedure that is never medically necessary and should be prohibited."[73] In press releases concerning the dismemberment abortion ban in Texas, Texas Right to Life uses similar language in favor of banning this method of killing preborn children.[74] They use phrases like "Particularly gruesome," "torturous," and "inhumane," all of which are true. But the reason for outlawing partial-birth abortions and dismemberment abortion is the same reason for outlawing all abortions. The reason is that all abortions are the unjust killing of an image bearer. The gruesome, torturous, inhumane methods are vile, but the *method* by which an image bearer is unjustly killed does not make the act more unjust. Texas Right to Life says

---

[71] Health and Safety Code Title 2. Health Subtitle H. Public Health Provisions Chapter 171 Abortion subchapter F sections 171.101-171.106, https://statutes.capitol.texas.gov/Docs/HS/htm/HS.171.htm.

[72] Health and Safety Code Title 2. Health Subtitle H. Public Health Provisions Chapter 171 Abortion subchapter G sections 171.151-171.154 Https://statutes.capitol.texas.gov/Docs/HS/htm/HS.171.htm.

[73] Partial birth abortion act 2003 https://www.gpo.gov/fdsys/pkg/PLAW-108publ105/html/PLAW-108publ105.htm.

[74] These Texas Right to Life articles are quite telling of the secular Pro-Life establishment mindset over all.
https://www.texasrighttolife.com/governor-abbott-signs-dismemberment-abortion-ban-into-law/.
https://www.texasrighttolife.com/district-judge-order-places-hold-on-dismemberment-abortion-ban/.

about this law, "With the strong amendments added to SB 8, lives of the preborn will be saved and Texas will move forward in undermining the legal foundation of *Roe v. Wade*, the Supreme Court decision that legalized abortion in the United States."[75] Focusing on the brutality of some methods of killing preborn children over others is dehumanizing to those killed in "less gruesome," "less torturous," and "more humane" methods. This subverts their agenda to undermine the legal foundation of the unconstitutional ruling by recognizing its legitimacy, working within its stated bounds, and codifying it. Regulating *how* preborn children are killed still effectively sanctions the practice of killing preborn children.

Several abortuaries filed a restraining order against this Pro-Life legislative victory, SB8. Here are some quotes from the *Transcript Of Hearing On Request For Temporary Restraining Order* where Darren Mccarty, Pro-Life lawyer for Texas Attorney General office, is defending this piece of Pro-Life legislation.

> Good morning, Your Honor,
> Darren McCarty for the Attorney General. Unlike Plaintiffs have indicated, SB8 is not a ban on D&E. SB8 is measured piece of legislation that does not require nor is it intended to create a substantial obstacle to second trimester abortion. In fact, the plaintiffs, despite submitting evidence, despite waiting to file their case until later, have not presented any evidence in the record that SB8 would

[75] Ibid.

> bar a single woman in Texas from receiving an abortion. Not one.[76]

In defending this Pro-Life legislation, the Pro-Life Attorney General Office admits that this law will not bar a single woman in Texas from receiving an abortion, yet the secular Pro-Life organizations say that because of this law "lives of the preborn will be saved." The Pro-Life Attorney General continues to say this:

> SB8 is designed to do one thing and one thing only, and that is to end the particularly brutal, gruesome, and inhumane practice of killing a second trimester, essentially fully formed fetus by tearing it apart limb from limb. Texas has decided that these unborn children are entitled to more dignity. SB8 reflects the ethos of a humane and civilized society. SB8 would require one thing, a humane termination of an unborn child's life before it is dismembered and evacuated.
>
> That's all it does.[77]

He is stating that this Pro-Life legislation does not stop any killing of the preborn. In fact, the Pro-Life legislation does not even stop the dismembering of the preborn person.

---

[76] TRANSCRIPT OF HEARING ON REQUEST FOR TEMPORARY RESTRAINING ORDER BEFORE THE HONORABLE LEE YEAKEL Case 1:17-cv-00690-LY Document 61 Filed 09/05/17 Page 20.

[77] TRANSCRIPT OF HEARING ON REQUEST FOR TEMPORARY RESTRAINING ORDER BEFORE THE HONORABLE LEE YEAKEL Case 1:17-cv-00690-LY Document 61 Filed 09/05/17 Page 21.

You can still kill this preborn child. You can even dismember this preborn child, as long as you kill the preborn child *before* you dismember him/her. Again, these are the words of the Pro-Life Attorney General defending this strong Pro-Life legislation. He reiterates his claim minutes later.

There is no doubt that D&E of a living infant in the womb is gruesome. It's brutal, and it's inhumane. The State has a legitimate interest. It has passed a marginal, moderate remedy that simply asks the plaintiffs to do what they are already doing by their own admission in many cases, and that is inducing fetal demise prior to –prior to, Your Honor, the dismemberment of the child and evacuation from the uterus. [78]

The secular Pro-Life establishment is also proud of their success in writing, endorsing, and passing various informed consent laws.[79] These laws are basically a check-list of things that the abortionist and the woman procuring the abortion must do before the state allows them to kill a preborn child. In Texas a mother can kill her preborn child 24 hours after signing this form listing the necessary requirements. The state of Texas sanctions the homicide of the preborn child as long as the mother is given printed papers or sent to a website that details medical risks from both abortion and carrying the child to birth, public and private agencies that provide options other than the killing of her child, and medical

[78] TRANSCRIPT OF HEARING ON REQUEST FOR TEMPORARY RESTRAINING ORDER BEFORE THE HONORABLE LEE YEAKEL Case 1:17-cv-00690-LY Document 61 Filed 09/05/17 Page 34.

[79] SUBCHAPTER B. INFORMED CONSENT 171.011-171.018 https://statutes.capitol.texas.gov/Docs/HS/htm/HS.171.htm.

assistance programs, among other things. The state of Texas sanctions the homicide of the preborn child as long as the mother has a sonogram and waits 24 hours after completing its check-list.[80] These types of informed consent laws are in all states with minor variations.

> ABORTION AND SONOGRAM ELECTION
> (1) The information and printed materials described by sections 171.012 (a) (1)-(3), Texas health and safety code, have been provided and explained to me.
> (2) I understand the nature and consequences of an abortion.
> (3) Texas law requires that I receive a sonogram prior to receiving an abortion.
> (4) I understand that I have the option to view the sonogram images.
> (5) I understand that I have the option to hear the heartbeat.
> (6) I understand that I am required by law to hear an explanation of the sonogram images unless I certify in writing to one of the following:
> —I am pregnant as a result of a sexual assault, incest, or other violation of the Texas penal code that has

[80] There is a huge irony of these informed consent laws and Mens Rea of abortive mothers described in the last chapter. The secular Pro-Life establishment writes laws that force women to see an ultrasound in order to show that it's a baby, and then they force a waiting period to think about the baby they are going to kill. Once these women kill their preborn children the same secular Pro-Life establishment says that they don't have the necessary intent and knowledge to prosecute for criminal homicide.

been reported to law enforcement authorities or that has not been reported because I reasonably believe that doing so would put me at risk of retaliation resulting in serious bodily injury.

—I am a minor and obtaining an abortion in accordance with judicial bypass procedures under *Chapter* 33, Texas family code.

—My fetus has an irreversible medical condition or abnormality, as identified by reliable diagnostic procedures and documented in my medical file.

(7) I am making this election of my own free will and without coercion.

(8) For a woman who lives 100 miles or more from the nearest abortion provider that is a facility licensed under *Chapter 245* or a facility that performs more than 50 abortions in any 12-month period only: I certify that, because I currently live 100 miles or more from the nearest abortion provider that is a facility licensed under chapter 245 or a facility that performs more than 50 abortions in any 12-month period, I waive the requirement to wait 24 hours after the sonogram is performed before receiving the abortion procedure. My place of residence is:__________.

Signature__________

DATE__________[81]

[81] 171.012 subdivision (5) https://statutes.capitol.texas.gov/Docs/HS/htm/HS.171.htm.

Almost all these secular Pro-Life laws have exceptions. These exceptions fail to apply equal justice and undermine their agenda (to make abortion unthinkable) by acting contrary to that assertion. The most commonly discussed exceptions are rape and incest. Rape and incest are violent crimes that should be investigated, adjudicated, and the perpetrators should be punished accordingly. These actions are detestable, and as Christians we ought to seek for justice on behalf of the victims. In these crimes, the body of a weaker image bearer is violated, against their will, by one that is stronger. This is not unlike abortion itself, in which a stronger person violates the body of a weaker person, against their will, to death. These so-called hard cases, according to Guttmacher, have fluctuated over the past 30 years between 0.5% and 1% of procured abortions. Even though the number of occurrences is extremely low, the emotional charge connected to these crimes gains them a great deal of attention. For this reason, nearly all of the secular Pro-Life laws that regulate the killing of preborn children through abortion have exceptions for rape and incest written into them.

These exceptions, like all the aforementioned secular Pro-Life laws, are also unjust for the same reason. In rightly wanting to show compassion and support for victims of such horrible crimes, they have once again dehumanized some preborn children, this time because they were conceived by a heinous act. Rape and incest exceptions expose the sin of partiality by denying that the dignity, value, and worth of a human is solely connected to the image of God. In doing so, they grant the execution of children for the crimes of their fathers.

The secular Pro-Life establishment rightly wants to save preborn babies from being killed by their parents. Their zeal for this is admirable, but their legal strategy and its implementation is inconsistent. Their focus on carnal results blinds them to consistent and appropriate methodology. Ironically, they fail to achieve even the desired results. The unjust laws that the secular Pro-Life establishment writes, promotes, and passes are often defended by their supporters with the claim that they want to save as many babies as possible. Their utilitarian approach is rooted in situational ethics and moral relativism. They nearly universally justify these unjust laws by quoting Matthew 10:16, "be wise as serpents." We are commanded to be as wise, or shrewd, as serpents. We are not, however, commanded to *be* serpents nor to act like them. Rather, we are commanded in the same verse to be innocent as doves. Not once has the rest of the verse been quoted when Pro-Life adherents have said to me, countless times in their rationalization for supporting unjust laws, "be wise as serpents." In fact, when I counter their argument by finishing the verse, admonishing them not to be serpents, they always look dumbfounded.

WHAT HAS GOD SAID ABOUT INIQUITOUS DECREES

Let us start by thinking back to what was said in chapter 1 about the work of God's providence and remember His intimate dealings with His creation. God the good Creator of all things, in his infinite power and wisdom doth **uphold, direct, dispose, and govern all creatures and things**, from the greatest even to the least, by his most wise and holy providence, to the end for the which they were created, according unto his infallible foreknowledge, and the free and immutable counsel of his own will; to the praise of the glory of his wisdom, power, justice, infinite goodness, and mercy.[82] The Christian finds comfort in the sovereign care, control, and preservation which our God exerts over His creation as He moves history forward to its telos. Each detail is crafted with precision to glorify Him. Now we will focus on the implications of biblical texts that deal with the providential control God exerts over the civil magistrate and, consequently, the laws they adjudicate.

As we work through the text of Scripture, recognize how beautifully God reveals His sovereign care and control in providence. It is not contingent on His creation, but rather He brings it about by establishing secondary causes and making use of means in providence. This is how He moves the created order through history.[83] All that to say that God, according to the counsel of His good pleasure, does uphold, direct, dispose, and govern all creatures and things by establishing means and using them, including the choices of sinful man, in harmony.

Let every person be subject to the governing authorities. For there is no authority except from God, and those that exist have been instituted by God. Therefore whoever resists the authorities resists what God has appointed, and those who resist will incur judgment. For rulers are not a terror to good conduct, but to bad. Would you have no fear of the one who

---

[82] Second London Baptist Confession of Faith, 5.1. Emphasis mine.

[83] Second London Baptist Confession of Faith Chapters 3 and 5 are very helpful here.

is in authority? Then do what is good, and you will receive his approval, for he is God's servant for your good. But if you do wrong, be afraid, for he does not bear the sword in vain. For he is the servant of God, an avenger who carries out God's wrath on the wrongdoer. Therefore one must be in subjection, not only to avoid God's wrath but also for the sake of conscience. "For because of this you also pay taxes, for the authorities are ministers of God, attending to this very thing." (Romans 13:1-6, ESV).

God has ordained and appointed all civil magistrates. They are His servants, His deacons. The primary function of these rulers is to wield the sword of justice on God's behalf. Take a moment to think back on what was said about this sword of truth and justice in chapter 1. This two-edged sword from the mouth of our Lord is the standard by which judgment is made. It is universal, unchanging and, will stand forever as it judges with perfection. this standard, which we will be judged by, is also the very standard we are commanded to use in our judgments as image bearers. As God's servant of justice, the king/civil magistrate is the Genesis 9:6 avenger of blood who carries out God's wrath on the wrongdoer with this sword[84]

"And for your lifeblood I will require a reckoning: from every beast I will require it and from man. From his fellow man I

[84] I found this article very helpful in connecting the civil magistrate of Romans 13 to Genesis 9:6. Power to the people: Revisiting Civil Resistance in Romans 13:1-7 in light of the Noahic Covenant by David Vandrunen, Journal of Law and Religion 31, no. 1, 2016.

will require a reckoning for the life of man. Whoever sheds the blood of man, by man shall his blood be shed, for God made man in his own image." (Genesis 9:5-6, ESV).

Much may be gathered from these two verses, but we will concentrate on the most obvious implications. First, Moses records God's words, which have the creation account in mind. The culmination of God's creative act is man in His image and likeness, showing the value of life that God has placed on him through His image. This is restated in the Noahic covenant which requires a reckoning for the life of man who is made in His image. This is the essence of what it means to be human, the image of God. The accidental qualities of each individual human does not give them value.[85] The second observation is that this retributive justice is to be judged by man, who is made in God's own image (the last phrase of v. 6). Man is to image God and judge accordingly. Think back to chapter 1 and apply retributive justice as the blood avenger.[86] This is the definition of God's appointed servant that the apostle Paul has in mind in Romans 13. Because man is created in the image of God, he (the civil magistrate) is to judge according to that image and apply retributive justice; he carries out God's wrath on the wrongdoer, and does not bear the sword that he is entrusted with in vain, lest he too fall under that same sword.[87]

---

[85] This was the argument of the last chapter on equal justice and is vital in its application to this chapter.
[86] This is a very good article by Brandon Adams on the blood avenger. Follow the links within the article for further study. http://reformedlibertarian.com/articles/theology/the-avenger-of-blood/.
[87] Foreshadowing.

Notice that the institution of the blood avenger, who wields the sword of justice and with it (God's wrath on the wrongdoer), is embedded in the Noahic covenant. In the first chapter, we said that this covenant was imposed, not just on Noah or his children, but all the flesh of the earth and in fact every living creature. It is common to both the elect and the reprobate. Part of the preservation of man in this covenant is through the avenger of blood and the retributive justice that he wields as God's servant. The law of retributive justice is given to believers and unbelievers alike in this preserving covenant. Understanding how the sword-bearing, wrath-bringing appointed servant of God is tied to God's command for justice in the Noahic covenant of preservation helps us make sense of its universal nature.[88] It shows the care and control God exerts in providence to preserve creation, and in that, His people.

A biblical example of a pagan magistrate appointed by God to bear His sword of justice is Cyrus. He was prophesied in Isaiah 45. In His providence, God established and used secondary means (this pagan king) to move history forward to its ordained end. Consider how this king brings justice and the wrath of God on the wrongdoer in his judgments, in this case against other kings and nations, including Babylon.

> Thus says the Lord to his anointed, to Cyrus, whose right hand I have grasped, to subdue nations before him and to loose the belts of kings, to open doors before him that gates may not be closed: I will go

[88] The civil magistrate and her laws are common to both believers and unbelievers alike.

before you and level the exalted places, I will break in pieces the doors of bronze and cut through the bars of iron, I will give you the treasures of darkness and the hoards in secret places, that you may know that it is I, the Lord, the God of Israel, who call you by your name. For the sake of my servant Jacob, and Israel my chosen, I call you by your name, I name you, though you do not know me. I am the Lord, and there is no other, besides me there is no God; I equip you, though you do not know me, that people may know, from the rising of the sun and from the west, that there is none besides me; I am the Lord, and there is no other. I form light and create darkness; I make well-being and create calamity; I am the Lord, who does all these things.

Shower, O heavens, from above, and let the clouds rain down righteousness; let the earth open, that salvation and righteousness may bear fruit; let the earth cause them both to sprout; I the Lord have created it. "Woe to him who strives with him who formed him, a pot among earthen pots! Does the clay say to him who forms it, 'What are you making?' or 'Your work has no handles'? Woe to him who says to a father, 'What are you begetting?' or to a woman, 'With what are you in labor?' " Thus says the Lord, the Holy One of Israel, and the one who formed him: "Ask me of things to come; will you command me concerning my children and the work of my hands? I made the earth and created man on it; it was my hands that stretched out the heavens, and I

> commanded all their host. I have stirred him up in righteousness, and I will make all his ways level; he shall build my city and set my exiles free, not for price or reward," says the Lord of hosts. (Isaiah 45:1-13, ESV).

God has explained these general principles to us in Proverbs 21. The king, as God's instrument of justice, converges and concurs with His sovereign providence. The earthly king is to judge with appropriate image bearing, and he is to do so with equal scales of weights and measures. Recall what was said in the last chapter about the equal application of justice and that the laws themselves must also be just. Verse 7 states what happens when the king fails to properly image God as His blood avenging servant.

> The king's heart is a stream of water in the hand of the Lord; he turns it wherever he will.
> Every way of a man is right in his own eyes, but the Lord weighs the heart.
> To do righteousness and justice is more acceptable to the Lord than sacrifice.
> Haughty eyes and a proud heart, the lamp of the wicked, are sin.
> The plans of the diligent lead surely to abundance, but everyone who is hasty comes only to poverty. The getting of treasures by a lying tongue is a fleeting vapor and a snare of death.

> The violence of the wicked will sweep them away, because they refuse to do what is just. (Proverbs 21:1-7).

I would like to turn our attention to a specific example of God using a civil magistrate in His providence. God is the one who changes the times and epochs. He removes kings and establishes kings. Each successive civil magistrate is the judgment of his predecessor's failure to execute justice with precision. He falls to violence and is swept away in judgment because of his refusal to do what is just. This can take the form of unjust actions, bearing the sword in vain or even sinful motivations behind the proper action. Isaiah 10 starts with an indictment against the nation of Israel for their lack of equal justice in the writing and application of their laws.

> Woe to those who decree iniquitous decrees, and the writers who keep writing oppression, to turn aside the needy from justice and to rob the poor of my people of their right, that widows may be their spoil, and that they may make the fatherless their prey! What will you do on the day of punishment, in the ruin that will come from afar? To whom will you flee for help, and where will you leave your wealth? Nothing remains but to crouch among the prisoners or fall among the slain. For all this his anger has not turned away, and his hand is stretched out still. (Isaiah 10:1-4, ESV).

We are not, as we have said, the nation of Israel after the flesh. However, the admonition and principles found here are of benefit to all common kingdom nations. The charges levied against Israel are a warning to all. Those who made iniquitous decrees were in violation of their Noahic covenant duties as the sword of justice bearing servants of God. This warning goes to all who now write, support, and pass unjust laws that oppress the majority of the preborn and also to those who apply these laws without equal justice. Following the declaration of guilt, God lays out the earthly punishment. He is raising up a king to be the rod of His anger, the next blood avenger to bring His wrath on the wrongdoer. He is appointing the next sword-bearing civil magistrate to be the axe in His hand. Retributive justice is coming on a national level at the hands of a foreign conquering king, who will also fall for his own unjust motivations and iniquitous decrees. Our American history of injustice towards our image bearing brothers and sisters demands the faithful right arm of the Lord executed through His chosen instruments.

> Woe to Assyria, the rod of my anger; the staff in their hands is my fury!
> Against a godless nation I send him, and against the people of my wrath I command him, to take spoil and seize plunder, and to tread them down like the mire of the streets.
> But he does not so intend, and his heart does not so think; but it is in his heart to destroy, and to cut off nations not a few; for he says: "Are not my commanders all kings?

Is not Calno like Carchemish?
Is not Hamath like Arpad?
Is not Samaria like Damascus?
As my hand has reached to the kingdoms of the idols, whose carved images were greater than those of Jerusalem and Samaria, "shall I not do to Jerusalem and her idols as I have done to Samaria and her images?"
When the Lord has finished all his work on Mount Zion and on Jerusalem, he will punish the speech of the arrogant heart of the king of Assyria and the boastful look in his eyes. For he says: "By the strength of my hand I have done it, and by my wisdom, for I have understanding; I remove the boundaries of peoples, and plunder their treasures; like a bull I bring down those who sit on thrones. [14]My hand has found like a nest the wealth of the peoples; and as one gathers eggs that have been forsaken, so I have gathered all the earth; and there was none that moved a wing
or opened the mouth or chirped."
Shall the axe boast over him who hews with it, or the saw magnify itself against him who wields it?
As if a rod should wield him who lifts it, or as if a staff should lift him who is not wood!
Therefore the Lord God of hosts will send wasting sickness among his stout warriors, and under his glory a burning will be kindled, like the burning of fire.

> The light of Israel will become a fire, and his Holy One a flame, and it will burn and devour his thorns and briers in one day.
> The glory of his forest and of his fruitful land
> the Lord will destroy, both soul and body,
> and it will be as when a sick man wastes away.
> The remnant of the trees of his forest will be so few that a child can write them down. (Isaiah 10:5-19, ESV).

God pronounces judgement against violations of His Noahic Covenant commands for equal justice. In His governance through providence, He uses His established servants to be His arm and execute His wrath on the wrongdoer. Next, we will see His woeful declarations of guilt against their justification of these unjust laws, for they listened to the lying lips of the serpent which deviate from what God has said. In a godly desire to save preborn babies' lives, many have turned to calling the wicked iniquitous decrees mentioned in this chapter *good*. We can praise God for every child's life that was spared by these unjust laws, but we cannot call these evil laws good laws.

> Woe to those who call evil good
> and good evil, who put darkness for light
> and light for darkness, who put bitter for sweet
> and sweet for bitter!
> Woe to those who are wise in their own eyes, and shrewd in their own sight!

> Woe to those who are heroes at drinking wine, and valiant men in mixing strong drink, [23]who acquit the guilty for a bribe, and deprive the innocent of his right!
> Therefore, as the tongue of fire devours the stubble, and as dry grass sinks down in the flame, so their root will be as rottenness, and their blossom go up like dust; for they have rejected the law of the Lord of hosts, and have despised the word of the Holy One of Israel.
> Therefore, the anger of the Lord was kindled against his people, and he stretched out his hand against them and struck them, and the mountains quaked; and their corpses were as refuse in the midst of the streets. For all this his anger has not turned away, and his hand is stretched out still. (Isaiah 5:20-25)

CONCLUSION

When you read these secular Pro-Life victories—laws that legislate, govern, direct, and control which preborn children women can kill, the acceptable methods by which they can kill them, the reasons women can kill them, and the simple tasks they must undertake before they kill their preborn children—do you hear the voice of the serpent asking, "Did God really say not to call evil good? ... Did God really pronounce woe against iniquitous decrees that pervert justice and indirectly write further oppression? ... Did God really say that He demands a reckoning for life taken? ... Did God really say not to be shrewd in your own sight and wise in your own eyes? ... Did God really say to be innocent as doves and apply equal weights and measures? ... Did God really say He would stretch out His arm against those in violation of His Noahic Covenant demands?"

Beloved in Christ, you have been given the mind of our risen Lord and are being transformed into His image. By the work of the gospel in your life, you can stand with Him on His word and say, as He did, "Thus says the Lord". The secular Pro-Life position is not the Christian position when it comes to writing and supporting legislation in the murder of the preborn. The laws that they write, promote, support, and celebrate are unjust. They are grounded in a worldview of moral relativism that is a denial of the absolute truth of God's word. We do not need new laws; we need only to equally apply the current homicide laws. At all costs, at all times, in all places, we are commanded to say with confidence, "Thus says the Lord."

Any law that sanctions the unjust killing of any human is objectively immoral. The law itself is objectively unjust and evil. Professing Christians will generally support incremental legislation in abortion because of a godly desire to prevent the unjust killing of some children. These same professing Christians will usually speak out against the antichristian philosophy that says the ends justify the means. In this instance however, they will compromise their stance on God's unchanging word about justice and justify it with the ends that some children may be saved from the slaughter. They are willing to forsake the revealed word of God and chase after the gods of this world and their antichristian worldview of moral relativism and situational ethics. We should hear Paul in Romans 3:8, "And why not *say* (as we are slanderously reported and as some claim that we say), 'Let us do evil that good may come'? Their condemnation is just." For example, when presented with a proposal of a 22 week ban on abortion, the Christian is duty bound to call it immoral, unjust, and evil. We do this by comparing this law, that sanctions the unjust killing of humans younger than 22 weeks in gestation, against God's objective unchanging standard of justice. Sadly, the majority of professing Christians do not. Instead they apply situational ethics and toss out the objective standard of God's morality. The secular prolife doctrine is not Christian. In fact, it is antichristian. They cannot tell you if a 22 week ban is good or evil of itself, but must first place it in the context of its current situation. To them it is a good law in, say, New York, that permits abortion throughout the gestational period. They would say this law in that situation saves some babies. The very same bill proposed in the context of the current Texas situation would be considered bad or evil by the secular prolife establishment because the government only sanctions the murder of children under 20 weeks. We as Christians can rejoice that children are prevented from being killed by these unjust laws, but it is not the Christian position to support such evil. The Christian ought to say that the law is objectively unjust. We need to look at the worldview that drives actions. Situational ethics and moral relativism is opposed to the Christian worldview of objective moral truth. May God grant us repentance and give us the courage and faith to leave this ungodly worldview behind, as we stand on His objective truth as the standard of our obedience and discernment of good and evil.

Tom Ascol, in a lecture on principles of biblical justice, says,

To do justice means we must treat people lawfully, impartiality, proportionately, and equitably. And where we see these principles being violated, brothers and sisters, we must stand up; we must call foul; we must speak out. and when Christians call for justice, they must make sure that what they calling for meets this criteria for biblical justice.[89]

As Christians, we must continually be conforming to the word of God. Any deviation in our application of its teaching is sin, and we must repent. As priests in the kingdom of God, we are required to consistently apply a Christian ethic—the word of God—to all our dealings in this world. This includes the laws we write, support, and pass. We must call evil out for the evil it is, and we must not call it good. May God grant us repentance and conform us more to the image of His Son and the truth of His word. We must lay down this sinful secular Pro-Life doctrine that denies equal justice for the preborn. We must remain innocent as doves in our fight against this injustice.

[89] https://youtu.be/8yebJ7uhgsE.

DOCTRINE OF LESSER MAGISTRATE: DEFY TYRANTS

In this chapter we will continue interacting with the second uncompromising pillar of the secular Pro-Life establishment: its long-term legal strategy to stop the killing of unborn children through abortion. In the last chapter we considered their intention to regulate abortion to the fullest extent by, and in a manner consistent with, the decisions of SCOTUS. In this chapter we will engage with the second part of that long-term legal strategy. The basis of this plan is to reverse the *Roe v. Wade* decision by changing the political climate and makeup of the court. We will look at the history, development, and effectiveness of what we will call civil idolatry. We will then look at the doctrine of the lesser magistrate and historical, extrabiblical examples of defying tyrants. Finally, we will see what God has said about Christians' duty to the civil magistrate.

CIVIL IDOLATRY OF THE SUPREME COURT

In the last chapter we briefly laid out the myth of judicial supremacy, which undergirds the secular Pro-Life philosophy of writing legislation that complies with the dictates of the tyrannical court. Unwavering belief in this myth is what drives the secular Pro-Life establishment to the second part of their long-term legal strategy. Through most of the 1970s, their main strategy was to create a constitutional amendment declaring life and personhood from conception, affording the preborn child the same God-given, constitutional rights and protections as the born. After a few years of failed attempts due to lack of support, the strategy shifted to reversing the decision of the court by changing the makeup of the court. The idea is to support Republican Pro-Life presidential candidates who would nominate Republican Pro-Life justices. Once the court has been filled with Republican Pro-Life appointed justices, then *Roe v. Wade* can be reversed. This strategy itself feeds the myth of judicial supremacy and enshrines the expanding power of SCOTUS, bowing to the court and their unjust rulings. This is the definition of civil idolatry. Let's take a historical look at the past 45 years and see the development of the court and the effectiveness of this strategy.

The *Roe v. Wade* decision was a 7-2 vote. Voting for this unjust ruling were two Democrat justices: (Douglas and Marshall) and five Republican justices (Burger, Brennan, Stewart, Blackmun, and Powel). Voting against the ruling were Republican justice Rehnquist and Democrat justice White. The 1973 ruling was made by a predominantly Republican court.

Voting For	Voting Against
(D) Douglas	(R) Rehnquist
(D) Marshall	(D)White

Voting For
(R) Burger
(R) Brennan
(R) Stewart
(R) Blackmun
(R) Powel

The first change to the Supreme Court came when Republican President Ford appointed Justice (R) Stevens to replace (D) Douglass, who had initially voted for the Roe decision. (R) Ronald Reagan ran on a Pro-Life platform, promising to appoint justices that would overturn the court's *Roe v. Wade* decision. As the elected Pro-Life president, he replaced (R) Stewart, (R) Powel, and (R) Burger, all of whom voted for the *Roe v. Wade* decision, with (R) O'Connor, (R) Kennedy, and (R) Scalia. (R) George Bush also ran on a Pro-Life platform, promising to appoint justices to overturn the court's *Roe v. Wade* decision. He replaced (R) Brennan and (D) Marshall, both of whom voted for *Roe v. Wade*, with (R) Souter and (R) Thomas. Over a 19-year period, Americans voted for Pro-Life presidents who appointed six justices to overturn *Roe v. Wade*. That was the strategy and the promises made by secular Pro-Life establishment and the candidates they supported. There was only one remaining justice that had voted for *Roe v. Wade*, two that had voted against it, and six new justices appointed by Pro-Life Republican presidents. In 1992, an opportunity to overturn the decision appeared with *Planned Parenthood v. Casey*. The court, dominated by Pro-Life Republican appointed justices, upheld and tightened the *Roe v. Wade* decision.

Voting For	Voting Against
(R) Blackmun	(D)White
(R) Stevens	(R) Scalia
(R) O'Connor	(R) Thomas
(R) Kennedy	(R) Rehnquist
(R) Souter	

The secular Pro-Life establishment focused much of its resources, time, and money on this long-term legal strategy to reverse the *Roe v. Wade* decision. The plan was to educate and support Republican Pro-Life candidates who would appoint Republican Pro-Life justices who would overturn *Roe v. Wade*. The plan was largely successful in electing Pro-Life presidents; it failed miserably when the justices voted to uphold and strengthen the unjust decision in *Planned Parenthood v. Casey*. The Pro-Life establishment renewed their efforts and resources in this dismal failure of a tactic.

In the following years, Democrat President Clinton replaced (D) White, the only Democrat justice voting against, with (D) Ginsberg. He then replaced (R) Blackmun, who voted for, with (D) Breyer. Republican President George W. Bush ran on a Pro-Life platform and replaced (R) Rehnquist, who voted against, and (R) O'Connor, who voted for, with (R) Roberts and (R) Alito. Democrat President Obama replaced (R) Stevens and (R) Souter, both of whom voted to uphold *Roe v. Wade* with (D) Sotomayor and (D) Kagan.

In 2016 Republican Donald Trump ran for president on a Pro-Life platform, promising to appoint Republican Pro-Life justices who would overturn the unjust decision. As a candidate, he caused a big stir with both the Pro-abortion crowd as well as the Pro-Life establishment. Not knowing the secular Pro-Life positions, he made comments consistent with thinking that abortion is homicide and should be criminalized. Many of the quotes used in chapter 2 came from secular Pro-Life organizations/leaders refuting his remarks. He quickly recanted and was educated on the actual secular Pro-Life stance on criminalization. In his first two years in office, he replaced (R) Scalia, who voted against, and (R) Kennedy who voted for, with (R) Gorsuch and (R) Kavanaugh. There is a strong possibility of (D) Ginsberg retiring for health reasons soon, giving Pro-Life Republican Trump another opportunity to appoint a likeminded justice. Let's look at the current makeup of the court.

Voted For	**Voted Against**	**Likely For**	**Likely Against (according to strategy)**
	(R)Thomas	(D)Sotomayor	(R) Gorsuch
		(D) Kagan	(R)Kavanaugh
		(D) Breyer	(R) Roberts
		(D)Ginsberg	(R) Alito

Justice Clarence Thomas is the only current justice on the court who has made clear statements expressing his stance, such as the following, in his 1992 dissent to *Planned Parenthood v. Casey*. "We believe that Roe was wrongly decided, and that it can and should be overruled consistently with our traditional approach to stare decisis in constitutional cases."[90] He made similar statements in his minority opinion in *Gonzalez v. Carhart*. "I write separately to reiterate my view

---

[90] https://web.utk.edu/~scheb/decisions/Casey.htm.

that the Court's abortion jurisprudence, including *Casey [Planned Parenthood of Se. Pa. v. Casey*, 505 U.S. 833, 112 S. Ct. 2791 (1992)] and *Roe v. Wade*, 410 U. S. 113, 93 S. Ct. 705 (1973), has no basis in the Constitution."[91] He joined with both Justice Alito and Justice Roberts in several cases, but, due to these remarks, neither of them would concur with his opinions about the illegitimacy of *Roe v. Wade* and *Planned Parenthood v. Casey*.

Justice Alito wrote, in a memo, "No one seriously believes that the Court is about to overrule *Roe*. But the Court's decision to review [the Pennsylvania case] may be a positive sign." He continued, "By taking these cases, the Court may be signaling an inclination to cut back. What can be made of this opportunity to advance the goals of bringing about the eventual overruling of *Roe v. Wade* and, in the meantime, of mitigating its effects?"[92] When questioned about it in his confirmation hearing, he said,

> The things that I said in the 1985 memo were a true expression of my views at the time from my vantage point as an attorney in the Solicitor General's office. But that was 20 years ago, and a great deal has happened in the case law since then. *Thornburg* was decided and *Webster* and then *Casey* and a number of other decisions. So the stare decisis analysis would have to take account of that entire line of case law."
> Couple this with his statement on precedent: "*Roe v.*

---

[91] https://supreme.justia.com/cases/federal/us/550/124/.

[92] Quoted in Jeffrey Toobin, *The Nine: Inside the Secret World of the Supreme Court* (New York: Anchor Books, 2008), 19.

> *Wade* is an important precedent of the Supreme Court. It was decided in 1973. So, it's been on the books for a long time. It has been challenged on a number of occasions. The Supreme Court has reaffirmed the decision; sometimes on the merits; sometimes--in *Casey*--based on stare decisis.[93]

Justice Roberts has made similar comments and gone further by saying, "It is a jolt to the legal system when you overrule a precedent. Precedent plays an important role in promoting stability and evenhandedness...It is not enough that you may think the prior decision was wrongly decided."[94] He has shown particular concern about overruling settled precedents, which would compromise the Court's legitimacy and public reputation. This is especially true when the American population finds abortion to be favorable if restricted. All this to say that Justice Roberts, like Justice Alito, shows a propensity to continue chipping away at the abortion "right" rather than overturning the Court's decision's outright. In February of 2019, Justice Roberts became the new Kennedy by joining with the liberal side of the court to block

---

[93] Transcripts for the CONFIRMATION HEARING ON THE NOMINATION OF SAMUEL A. ALITO, JR. TO BE AN ASSOCIATE JUSTICE OF THE SUPREME COURT OF THE UNITED STATES, https://www.govinfo.gov/content/pkg/GPO-CHRG-ALITO/pdf/GPO-CHRG-ALITO.pdf.

[94] Transcript for the CONFIRMATION HEARING ON THE NOMINATION OF JOHN G. ROBERTS, JR. TO BE CHIEF JUSTICE OF THE UNITED STATES, https://www.judiciary.senate.gov/imo/media/doc/GPO-CHRG-ROBERTS.pdf.

a Louisiana abortion law which went beyond what is allowed by *Roe* and *Casey*.

This alone kills any chance of the current SCOTUS declaring the previous *Roe v. Wade/Planned Parenthood v. Casey* rulings unjust and void. Justice Gorsuch and Justice Kavanaugh are a little harder to pin down. However, they make similar remarks as Justices Alito and Roberts have made pertaining to the nature of the precedent established and reaffirmed in the illegitimate ruling. Justice Kavanaugh, in his confirmation hearing, said of the *Roe v. Wade* decision, "it is settled law... One of the important things to keep in mind about Roe vs. Wade is that it has been reaffirmed many times over the past 45 years... I will tell you what my view right now is, which is it's an important precedent of the Supreme Court that has been reaffirmed many times... The Supreme Court didn't just reaffirm it in passing."[95] Referring to *Planned Parenthood v. Casey* as "Precedent on Precedent" in 2006,[96] he says, "If confirmed to the D.C. Circuit, I would follow Roe v. Wade faithfully and fully... That would be binding precedent of the Court. It's been decided by the Supreme Court."[97] He, like Justice Roberts, is concerned that the legitimacy of SCOTUS could be called into question in a major overturning of earlier decision, eroding the expression of

---

[95] https://www.c-span.org/video/?449704-1/brett-kavanaugh-confirmation-hearing-begins-amid-democratic-objections-public-protests.
[96] Transcripts for the CONFIRMATION HEARING ON THE NOMINATION OF BRETT KAVANAUGH TO BE CIRCUIT JUDGE FOR THE DISTRICT OF COLUMBIA CIRCUIT, https://www.congress.gov/109/chrg/shrg27916/CHRG-109shrg27916.htm
[97] Ibid.

their judicial supremacy and the people's trust in the institution.

Following suit, Justice Gorsuch says, "Part of the value of precedent—and it has lots of value—it has value in and of itself, because it is our history and our history has value intrinsically... But it also has an instrumental value in this sense: it adds to the determinacy of law... Once a case is settled, that adds to the determinacy of law... What was once a hotly contested issue is no longer a hotly contested issue. We move forward."[98] In his confirmation hearing, Justice Gorsuch had the following exchange with Senator Durbin: "Senator, as the book explains, the Supreme Court of the United States has held in Roe v. Wade that a fetus is not a person for purposes of the Fourteenth Amendment, and the book explains that," "Do you accept that?" Durbin asked. "That's the law of the land," Gorsuch answered. "I accept the law of the land, senator, yes."[99]

Based on past opinions from these justices, I think a more accurate projection would look like this.

Voted For	Voted Against	Likely For	Likely Against
	(R)Thomas	(D)Sotomayor	
		(D) Kagan	
		(D) Breyer	

[98] Transcript for the CONFIRMATION HEARING ON THE NOMINATION OF HON. NEIL M. GORSUCH TO BE AN ASSOCIATE JUSTICE OF THE SUPREME COURT OF THE UNITED STATES, https://www.govinfo.gov/content/pkg/CHRG-115shrg28638/pdf/CHRG-115shrg28638.pdf.

[99] Ibid.

Likely For
(D)Ginsberg
(R) Gorsuch
(R)Kavanaugh
(R) Roberts
(R) Alito

For the past 45 years, SCOTUS has been dominated by justices nominated by Pro-Life Republican presidents. In fact, except for a six-month period when there was a tie while waiting for (R) Scalia to be replaced, they have been the majority the entire time. Let that sink in. Think of the secular Pro-Life establishment's long-term legal strategy to change the makeup of the court by appointed justices through Pro-Life Republican presidents. If we continue this trend of supporting Pro-Life Republican presidential candidates who will appoint justices to overthrow the *Roe V. Wade* decision, a realistic projection of when it will finally happen is *never*.

DOCTRINE OF THE LESSER MAGISTRATE

What has God said about how His children are to respond to the tyranny of His appointed servant of justice? Many have argued for the Pro-Life position covered in the last few chapters, appealing to Romans 13. They claim that the Christian should fully submit to God's appointed authority, even when that authority wields unrestrained exercise of power. They say we must submit to his despotic abuse because resistance to him is resistance to God. We will search the text of Scripture to see how we are to engage, with the mind of Christ, God's ordained blood avenging servant of justice when he commands something that God has forbidden or forbids something God commands. This is called the doctrine of the lesser magistrate. We will outline it by working through examples from history in the biblical text. We will also see this played out in extra-biblical church history. Finally, we will see its appearance on the pages of pagan history, for even they have understood this doctrine through the light of nature.

We have discussed in previous chapters the function of the Romans 13 servant of God. He is appointed by God to image Him by judging with that sword of justice. As the Genesis 9:6 avenger of blood, he is to carry out God's wrath on the wrongdoer. The Christian is to submit to him as unto the Lord, as he is the axe in the hand of our Lord. He is the earthly representative of God's justice. In the last chapter we talked about the justice that befalls him when he fails to wield that sword properly. These discrepancies and deviations in his laws and the proper application of them illustrate the ways in which the Romans 13 servant of God oversteps the authority he has been given. This collision of standards shows the treason and sedition of the civil magistrate in establishing himself as an authority above God. They will be judged for this, as we demonstrated in the last chapter. When the line is drawn, on which side will you stand?

Earlier, Paul says, "Do you not know that if you present yourselves to anyone as obedient slaves, you are slaves of the one whom you obey, either of sin which leads to death, or of obedience, which leads to righteousness?"[100] The civil magistrate is appointed by God for your good. When he is a

[100] Romans 6:16, ESV.

faithful representation of God through his authority, your submission to him, his laws, and his judgments is dutiful obedience to your God. When he departs from the parameters of his assigned authority, as a despotic self-driven master, to whom will the Christian give their obedience and allegiance? Will it be to sin or to righteousness? Will it be to justice or to injustice? Will it be to good or to evil? When the two are vying for your obedience, the one you obey is your master. Beloved, you must decide whether it is right in the sight of God to listen to them rather than to God. You must decide if you fear those who kill the body but cannot kill the soul, rather than him who can destroy both soul and body in hell. When the civil magistrate commands something that God has forbidden or forbids something God commands, you must choose whom you will serve. You must say with the Apostles, "We must obey God rather than men."

This type of civil disobedience is submission and obedience to God. When that civil disobedience is done to stand in the gap and protect another that is being oppressed by the tyrant, it is called interposition. The doctrine of the lesser magistrate is rooted in interposition. This is when a magistrate engages in this civil disobedience to interpose for the oppressed against the tyrant higher magistrate.

In short, "the lesser magistrate doctrine declares that when the superior or higher civil authority makes unjust/immoral laws or decree, the lesser or lower ranking civil authority has both a right and a duty to refuse obedience to that superior authority. If necessary, the lesser authorities even have the right and obligation to actively resist the superior authority."[101] First we will look at a few examples of civil disobedience, interposition by citizens, and the doctrine of the lesser magistrate from Scripture, starting with Exodus 1:15-17.

> Then the king of Egypt said to the Hebrew midwives, one of whom was named Shiphrah and the other Puah, "When you serve as midwife to the Hebrew women and see them on the birthstool, if it is a son, you shall kill him, but if it is a daughter, she shall live." But the midwives feared God and did not do as the king of Egypt commanded them, but let the male children live. (ESV).

Pharaoh, king of Egypt, was arguably the unrivaled potentate of the Ancient Near East. Here in God's word we see him command the midwives to the Hebrew slave women to kill all the male children as they are born. The civil magistrate is commanding what God has forbidden and forbidding what God has commanded in the Noahic covenant of preservation. This violates the command to be fruitful and multiply, as well as implied commands in the application of retributive justice against the unjust taking of human life. Fearing God, these midwives defied the tyrant king of Egypt in his overreach of authority and interposed on behalf of the male slave children. It was their duty to obey God and resist the evil command of the king.

---

[101] Matthew Trewhella, *The Doctrine of the Lesser Magistrates* (self-published, 2013, 2.

Then the high officials and the satraps sought to find a ground for complaint against Daniel with regard to the kingdom, but they could find no ground for complaint or any fault, because he was faithful, and no error or fault was found in him. Then these men said, "We shall not find any ground for complaint against this Daniel unless we find it in connection with the law of his God."

Then these high officials and satraps came by agreement to the king and said to him, "O King Darius, live forever! All the high officials of the kingdom, the prefects and the satraps, the counselors and the governors are agreed that the king should establish an ordinance and enforce an injunction, that whoever makes petition to any god or man for thirty days, except to you, O king, shall be cast into the den of lions. Now, O king, establish the injunction and sign the document, so that it cannot be changed, according to the law of the Medes and the Persians, which cannot be revoked." Therefore King Darius signed the document and injunction.
When Daniel knew that the document had been signed, he went to his house where he had windows in his upper chamber open toward Jerusalem. He got down on his knees three times a day and prayed and gave thanks before his God, as he had done previously. Then these men came by agreement and found Daniel making petition and plea before his God. Then they came near and said before the king, concerning the injunction, "O king! Did you not sign

> an injunction, that anyone who makes petition to any god or man within thirty days except to you, O king, shall be cast into the den of lions?" The king answered and said, "The thing stands fast, according to the law of the Medes and Persians, which cannot be revoked." Then they answered and said before the king, "Daniel, who is one of the exiles from Judah, pays no attention to you, O king, or the injunction you have signed, but makes his petition three times a day." (Daniel 6:4-13, ESV).

This is the well-known Bible story of Daniel and the lion's den. Daniel had risen to prominent political influence as a civil magistrate. Many of the other officials were jealous. They devised a plan to trick the king into making an iniquitous decree that Daniel would not be able to obey. The king established the ordinance that whoever makes petition to any god or man for the next thirty days would be thrown into the lion's den. Daniel knew the king had made this law that forbade him to do what God had commanded. Do not forget that Daniel was a magistrate and that this act of defiance was more than civil disobedience and interposition by a citizen, but rather an act of interposition by a magistrate. Daniel chose to fear God rather than man. Daniel was an obedient servant to Christ and fulfilled his duty in defiance of the king's decree. Standing with God, he got down on his knees three times a day and prayed, giving thanks before his God, as he had done previously. Knowing the earthly consequence to his actions, he resisted the evil law of the king and worshiped God.

> And Saul said to him, "Why have you conspired against me, you and the son of Jesse, in that you have given him bread and a sword and have inquired of God for him, so that he has risen against me, to lie in wait, as at this day?" Then Ahimelech answered the king, "And who among all your servants is so faithful as David, who is the king's son-in-law, and captain over your bodyguard, and honored in your house? Is today the first time that I have inquired of God for him? No! Let not the king impute anything to his servant or to all the house of my father, for your servant has known nothing of all this, much or little." And the king said, "You shall surely die, Ahimelech, you and all your father's house." And the king said to the guard who stood about him, "Turn and kill the priests of the Lord, because their hand also is with David, and they knew that he fled and did not disclose it to me." But the servants of the king would not put out their hand to strike the priests of the Lord. (1 Samuel 22:13-17, ESV).

King Saul was seeking to kill David. He was angered at Ahimelech and the priests of God that gave David shelter, food, and the sword of Goliath. King Saul issued an immoral/unjust order to his servants to kill all the priests that helped David. This order to kill God's priests was a command from the civil magistrate to do something God forbids. The servants, in duty and obedience to God, defy the king and interpose. Regardless of the earthly consequences, they stood with God and would not put out their hand to strike the priests of the Lord.

> Therefore at that time certain Chaldeans came forward and maliciously accused the Jews. They declared to King Nebuchadnezzar, "O king, live forever! You, O king, have made a decree, that every man who hears the sound of the horn, pipe, lyre, trigon, harp, bagpipe, and every kind of music, shall fall down and worship the golden image. And whoever does not fall down and worship shall be cast into a burning fiery furnace. There are certain Jews whom you have appointed over the affairs of the province of Babylon: Shadrach, Meshach, and Abednego. These men, O king, pay no attention to you; they do not serve your gods or worship the golden image that you have set up." (Daniel 3:8-12, ESV).

God raised up Hananiah, Azariah, and Mishael, three Jewish young men in captivity. With the Lord's hand upon them, they were appointed to positions of influence over the province of Babylon as civil magistrates. King Nebuchadnezzar had a golden image erected; when the music played, all the inhabitants were to bow and worship the idol. Failure to comply with the iniquitous decree of the king meant being cast into a burning fiery furnace. This pagan civil magistrate commanded what God had forbidden, and these young men stood obedient to God. Their defiance to the king and his immoral law was submission to the Almighty, as was their duty. Not fearing man that could only cast them into the fiery furnace which kills the body, they feared the Lord Jesus Christ, whom they served, instead. They stood on His word, regardless of the circumstance of the earthly consequences.

> Now when they saw the boldness of Peter and John, and perceived that they were uneducated, common men, they were astonished. And they recognized that they had been with Jesus. But seeing the man who was healed standing beside them, they had nothing to say in opposition. But when they had commanded them to leave the council, they conferred with one another, saying, "What shall we do with these men? For that a notable sign has been performed through them is evident to all the inhabitants of Jerusalem, and we cannot deny it. But in order that it may spread no further among the people, let us warn them to speak no more to anyone in this name." So they called them and charged them not to speak or teach at all in the name of Jesus. But Peter and John answered them, "Whether it is right in the sight of God to listen to you rather than to God, you must judge, for we cannot but speak of what we have seen and heard." (Acts 4:13-20, ESV).

Peter and John were preaching Christ. The Jewish leaders commanded them to stop. This is an immoral/unjust decree forbidding what God has commanded. The Apostles, standing with God and in obedience to Him, defy the tyranny of the civil magistrate and continue to preach.

> And when they had brought them, they set them before the council. And the high priest questioned them, saying, "We strictly charged you not to teach in this name, yet here you have filled Jerusalem with your teaching, and you intend to bring this man's blood upon us." But Peter and the apostles answered, "We must obey God rather than men. (Acts 5:27-29, ESV).

Throughout Church history, men of God have applied civil disobedience, interposition, and the doctrine of the lesser magistrate in various forms. When the higher civil authority has given an unjust/immoral command, forbidding what God has commanded, or commanding what God has forbidden, we see leaders of the church defying the tyrannical overstep of God's servant of justice, and often interposing on behalf of the people.

A second century document called *The Martyrdom of Polycarp*, attributed to the Apostolic Fathers, recounts the details of civil disobedience in church history. Polycarp was a disciple of the Apostle John and the ordained bishop of Smyrna. He was arrested for being an "atheist," which meant not worshiping the Roman gods, including Caesar. He was commanded by the civil magistrate to do what God had forbidden, to offer up incense, and profess that Caesar is Lord. He resisted the tyranny of God's appointed servant in civil disobedience. Polycarp laid down his life standing on the word of God and obedience to Him, when he defied the iniquitous decree of the civil magistrate. He met with our Lord outside the camp to bear His reproach.[102]

---

[102] This revision into modern English is by Richard Neil Shrout, adapted from J.B. Lightfoot's translation of *The Martyrdom of Polycarp.*

8:2 And he was met by Herod the captain of police and his father Nicetes, who also removed him to their carriage and tried to prevail upon him, seating themselves by his side and saying, "Why, what harm is there in saying, Caesar is Lord, and offering incense," with more to this effect, "and saving yourself?" But he at first gave them no answer. When however they persisted, he said, "I am not going to do what you counsel me."
8:3 Then they, failing to persuade him, uttered threatening words and made him dismount with speed, so that he bruised his shin, as he got down from the carriage. And without even turning round, he went on his way promptly and with speed, as if nothing had happened to him, being taken to the stadium; there being such a tumult in the stadium that no man's voice could be so much as heard.
9:1 But as Polycarp entered into the stadium, a voice came to him from heaven; "Be strong, Polycarp, and play the man." And no one saw the speaker, but those of our people who were present heard the voice. And at length, when he was brought up, there was a great tumult, for they heard that Polycarp had been apprehended.
9:2 When then he was brought before him, the proconsul asked whether he were the man. And on his confessing that he was, he tried to persuade him to a denial saying, "Have respect to your age," and other things in accordance therewith, as it is their habit to say, "Swear by the genius of Caesar; repent and say, 'Away with the atheists.'" Then Polycarp with solemn countenance looked upon the whole multitude of lawless heathen that were in the stadium, and waved his hand to them; and groaning and looking up to heaven he said, "Away with the atheists."
9:3 But when the magistrate pressed him hard and said, "Swear the oath, and I will release you; revile the Christ," Polycarp said, "Eighty-six years have I been His servant, and He has done me no wrong. How then can I blaspheme my King who saved me?"
10:1 But on his persisting again and saying, "Swear by the genius of Caesar," he answered, "If you suppose vainly that I will swear by the genius of Caesar, as you say, and feign that you are ignorant who I am, hear you plainly: I am a Christian. But if you would learn the doctrine of Christianity, assign a day and give me a hearing."

At the Diet of Worms in 1521, Martin Luther defended his books, position, and ideas against the evils plaguing the Roman Catholic church. When he was questioned and told to recant, he replied, "Unless I am convinced by the testimony of the Scriptures or by clear reason (for I do not trust either in the pope or in councils alone, since it is well known that they have often erred and contradicted themselves), I am bound by the Scriptures I have quoted and my conscience is captive to the Word of God. I cannot and will not recant anything, since it is neither safe nor right to go against conscience. May God help me. Amen."[103] This resulted in the Edict of Worms, a decree issued by The Holy Roman Emperor Charles V. The supreme civil magistrate made a law banning

---

10:2 The proconsul said, "Prevail upon the people." But Polycarp said, "As for yourself, I should have held you worthy of discourse; for we have been taught to render, as is proper, to princes and authorities appointed by God such honor as does us no harm; but as for these, I do not hold them worthy, that I should defend myself before them."
11:1 Whereupon the proconsul said: "I have wild beasts here and I will throw you to them, except you repent." But he said, "Call for them, for the repentance from better to worse is a change not permitted to us; but it is a noble thing to change from that which is improper to righteousness."
11:2 Then he said to him again, "If you despise the wild beasts, I will cause you to be consumed by fire, unless you repent." But Polycarp said: "You threaten that fire which burns for a season and after a little while is quenched: for you are ignorant of the fire of the future judgment and eternal punishment, which is reserved for the ungodly. But why do you delay? Come, do what you will."
12:1 Saying these things and more besides, he was inspired with courage and joy, and his countenance was filled with grace, so that not only did it not drop in dismay at the things which were said to him, but on the contrary the proconsul was astounded and sent his own herald to proclaim three times in the midst of the stadium, "Polycarp has confessed himself to be a Christian."

[103] Martin Brecht, *Martin Luther*. tr. James L. Schaaf, (Philadelphia: Fortress Press, 1985–93), 1:460.

the writings of Martin Luther and labeling him a heretic and enemy of the state.

> For this reason, we forbid anyone from this time forward to dare, either by words or by deeds, to receive, defend, sustain, or favor the said Martin Luther. On the contrary, we want him to be apprehended and punished as a notorious heretic, as he deserves, to be brought personally before us, or to be securely guarded until those who have captured him inform us, whereupon we will order the appropriate manner of proceeding against the said Luther. Those who will help in his capture will be rewarded generously for their good work.
>
> As for his accomplices, those who help or favor the said Martin in whatever manner or who show obstinacy in their perversity, not receiving absolution from the pope for the evils they have committed, we will also proceed against them and will take all of their goods and belongings, movable and fixed, with the help either of the judges in the area in which they reside or of our parliaments and councils at Malines or in other cities in which these events are made known. Action will be taken according to the desire of the accusers or of our fiscal procurators, but always according to the constitution and the laws, whether canon, civil, or divine, written against those who commit heresy or the crime of *lèse majesté* . These laws will be applied regardless of

> person, degree, or privilege if anyone does not obey our edict in every manner.[104]

Luther's benefactor was Prince Fredrick the Wise, Elector of Saxony, and lesser magistrate to Charles V the emperor of Rome. He interposed as a magistrate on behalf of Martin Luther in defiance of the unjust/immoral Edict of Worms. In spite of the possible punishment for treason, Prince Fredrick feared God more than he feared man. He disobeyed the order of the emperor, refusing to arrest Luther. In fact, to protect the Reformer, he faked his abduction and hid him out of sight.

A few decades later we see another example of the doctrine of the lesser magistrate applied. This time, in the Magdeburg Confession, the doctrine is laid out in text, defined, and defended. Because of the interposition of Prince Fredrick, Charles V failed for 25 years to impose the unjust Imperial Edict of Worms. During this time the reformation teaching of Luther spread. Luther died in 1546 and within months Charles V joined forces with Pope Paul III and proceeded to crush the Reformation in Germany by force. Then John Fredrick the magnanimous, losing the battle of Muhlberg to the papists, was captured. Because of the civil disobedience to the Holy Roman Empire, many of the Protestant church leaders were imprisoned. Charles imposed the Augsburg Interim in 1548, a decree that called for the

---

[104] Edict of Worms, May 25, 1521, http://www.crivoice.org/creededictworms.html.

return of the Protestants back to Papist doctrine and practice.[105]

Over the next two years, nearly all of the German churches accepted the terms of peace with Rome and compromise with the Emperor and the Pope. Only one city stood and resisted the tyranny of God's appointed servant when he overstepped his authority by forbidding what God has commanded, and commanding what God has forbidden. The city officials and church leaders of Magdeburg, as lesser magistrates, stood in the gap and interposed on behalf of the people. Together as good citizens in submission to Christ as Lord, they drew up the document known as the Magdeburg Confession. They laid out the articles of Christian doctrine and expounded the doctrine of the lesser magistrate, concerning resistance to the overreaching authority. They exhorted readers of the confession to join in the active resistance against the Emperor Charles V and the Pope, as their Christian duty required of them.

In a short time, the German Reformation was all but extinguished and the city of Magdeburg stood as the lone beacon on the hill. Their defiance of the civil authority in submission to our Lord subjected them to a 13-month siege.

---

[105] The Imperial Diet forced the following on German Protestants: 1) a return to the view of seven sacraments, 2) an establishment of the doctrine of transubstantiation, 3) an acknowledgment of the authority of the pope, and 4) a rejection of the doctrine of justification by faith alone. It conceded the following to the Protestants: 1) the right for Protestant clergy to marry, and 2) the right for Protestant laity to receive both elements of the Lord's Supper (in traditional Roman Catholicism the cup is reserved for the priesthood). Matthew Trewhella in the foreword to his translation of *The Magdeburg Confession* 1550 (self-published, 2012), xxxi.

Many lives were lost. But, through the providence of God and His special care for His church, Christian liberty was acknowledged by Emperor Charles V in 1552 and the Reformation continued to sweep the globe.

Theodore Beza was highly influenced by the doctrine of the lesser magistrate as expressed in the Magdeburg Confession and lived out by the interposition of the lesser magistrates of the city. This is apparent in his writing, as he took part in the French Wars of Religion in resistance to the tyranny of God's ordained servant of justice in France.[106]

John Knox used the Magdeburg Confession to help formulate his own writings to the lesser-magistrates of Scotland in his Appellation 1558. He pleaded with them to execute their duty to resist and defend against the Romish tyranny and protect the people from their oppressive, unjust decrees.

> True it is, God has commanded kings to be obeyed; but likewise true it is, that in things which they commit against His glory, He has commanded no obedience, but rather, He has approved, yea, and greatly rewarded, such as have opposed themselves to their ungodly commandments and blind rage.[107]

> You are bound to correct and repress whatsoever you know him (the higher magistrate) to attempt expressly repugning to God's word, honor, glory, or

---

[106] Theodor Beza, *Du droit des magistrats sur leurs subiets*, 1574.

[107] John Knox, *Selected Writings of John Knox*, edit Kevin Reed (Dallas, Tx: Presbyterian Heritage Publishing, 1558/1995), 504.

what you shall espy him to do against his subjects great or small.[108]

John Calvin said, "For earthly princes lay aside their power when they rise up against God and are unworthy to be reckoned among the number of mankind. We, ought rather, to spit upon their heads than to obey them." [109] Whereas Knox, Beza, and the Magdeburg confessors detailed and defended the doctrine focusing on special revelation, Calvin chose to focus on general revelation and show examples found in pagan history. This will further evidence what we have been saying about the image of God, justice, and how this doctrine is revealed in the light of nature.

Many of the 16th century Reformers used an anecdote from General Trajan when promoting and arguing for various forms of political resistance throughout Europe. Trajan rose to become Senatorial Emperor of Rome at the end of the first century. It is claimed that as he took power, he handed a sword to a recently appointed officer and made this declaration: "If I rule justly, use it by my side, If I rule unjustly, use it against me." To this day the military makes this same distinction in lawful and unlawful commands, and in the duty and responsibility of the lower ranking individual (lesser magistrate) to defy the unlawful commands of a superior officer.

In AD 40-41, we have a wonderful account of the doctrine of the lesser magistrate being applied by Petronius, Roman

---

[108] Ibid., 505.

[109] John Calvin, *Calvin's Bible commentaries, Daniel Vol 1-2*, (Edinburgh: Banner of truth, 1965).

Governor over Syria under Caligula the Emperor of Rome.[110] Caligula caused himself to be worshiped as a god throughout the Roman empire, resulting in unrest and revolt in Judea among the Jews. He commanded his statue to be placed in Jerusalem, in the Temple itself. The Jews were expected to violently resist. He ordered Petronius to enter Judea with two legions to crush any rebellion to the erection and worship of his statue in the temple. Seeking a peaceable resolution, Petronius entered into dialog with the Jews of Judea and those in Tiberias. Tens of thousands of Jews pleaded with Petronius. They are recorded as saying

> He would not compel them to transgress and violate the law of their forefathers. But if, said they, thou art entirely resolved to bring this statue, and erect it, do thou first kill us; and then do what thou hast resolved on. For while we are alive, we cannot permit such things as are forbidden us to be done, by the authority of our legislator; and by our forefathers determination that such prohibitions are instances of virtue.[111]

Petronius began a series of delay tactics, having the statue built in Sidon and then moved to Jerusalem. He also slowed its construction to buy more time. The unrelenting Jews,

---

[110] The incident of Petronius applying the doctrine of the lesser magistrate and interposing for the Jews against the unjust orders of emperor Caligula are recorded in Josephus, *Antiquities of the Jews Book XVIII*, chapter 8. It is also recorded by Philo in *Legatio ad Gaium*, §§ 30-34.
[111] Josephus, *Antiquities of the Jews, Book XVIII*, chapter 8.

claiming to die rather than have the temple defiled, moved Petronius to interpose at greater lengths on their behalf. He led his troops back to Antioch and wrote the emperor, entreating him to countermand his order.

The emperor, giving favor to king Agrippa, who now lived in Rome, ordered that the temple in Jerusalem undergo no alterations. Emperor Caligula was not earnest in this countermanded order. He recognized the delaying tactics of Petronius as appeasement to the Jews that were refusing to worship him.

The letter Petronius wrote to the emperor, interposing for the Jews, enraged him. Caligula ordered a statue of himself to be built and personally moved to Jerusalem to be worshiped in the temple. He reissued the invasion of Judea and violent annihilation of the revolting Jews, going back on all of the concessions made to king Agrippa. He wrote to Petronius, ordering him to kill himself for his disobedience, interposing for the Jews as the lesser magistrate.

> Seeing thou esteemest the presents made thee by the Jews to be of greater value than my commands; and art grown insolent enough to be subservient to their pleasure, I charge thee to become thy own judge; and to consider what thou art to do, now thou art under my displeasure. For I will make thee an example to the present, and to all future ages; that they may not dare to contradict the commands of their Emperor.[112]

---

[112] Josephus, *Antiquities of the Jews, Book XVIII*, chapter 8.

As the providence of God would have it, the Emperor was murdered shortly after the letter was sent. The news of Caligula's death reached Petronius before the letter ordering him to commit suicide as punishment for his insubordination.

In our final example from pagan history, we will enter the context of our American experiment. As we delve into this, take notice of its strong correlation to the topic of abortion and the duties of the lesser magistrate to defy tyrannical injustice and their enforcers. We should look back on our history with great sadness and concern that God's appointed blood avenging servant wielded the sword in vain. He stood in defiance of God, his responsibilities, and the founding documents of our country. He used the power of that sword entrusted him to dehumanize and oppress an entire class of people based on the accidental property[113] of ethnicity. The unjust, vain use of this sword demanded the execution of justice fall on him in judgment. We should also look back and be inspired by the courage and commitment of the few lesser magistrates that interposed in protection of the people against the sword wielding tyrant. Let us be grateful for the repentance granted by God, and continue with urgency and unwavering commitment to strive in it. Let us learn from the sins of our horrific past and apply the lessons, repenting of the sinful partiality we as a nation express in dehumanizing the preborn.

---

[113] Accidental properties are the attributes that are added to the essence of humanity that make an individual the unique instantiation of human that they are. The essence of humanity, that which what makes a creature human, is the image of God. The accidental properties, such as ethnicity, gender, age, height, weight, are the things that separate you from all other humans.

From its inception, our country has lived in perpetual cognitive dissonance. Our claim is that all men are created equal by God with rights endowed by Him on all. In order to justify our bloodlust greed, we institute programs of dehumanization against whatever class of people (discriminated by accidental properties) that we wish to exploit for gain. We continue to live in direct opposition to the ideological foundation of our nation, society, and God. Slavery is an obvious example of this sinful practice of injustice in our country and one for which we stand in judgment. Our nation categorized image bearers as chattel property and denied them the God-endowed rights we based our country on. We denied them citizenship, personhood, and all the protection of their God-given rights. By ignoring the ontological essence of humanity and the value of the image in which man is created, we focused on accidental properties, as if value comes from them.

A few pointed out this inconsistency, seeking justice against slavery. The union was fractured into free states and slave states—though deep rooted racism was everywhere in the middle of the 19th century. In an effort to be brief, let us consider just two threads of this atrocity, the unjust *Dread Scott v. Sandford* 1857 SCOTUS ruling and the evil *Fugitive Slave ACT* 1850.

Dred Scott was born a slave in 1795. A series of events, including being sold to an army surgeon, brought him to live in a few free states. He got married and had children in these free states. Scott attempted to purchase his family's freedom in 1846. When his owner refused, he took legal action. After years of appeals, the case reached SCOTUS. The court's abhorrent ruling made three assertions. First, black people could not be, nor were ever intended to be, citizens of the United States; therefore, they could not file suit in American court. Second, it labeled the Missouri Compromise unconstitutional, saying congress could not ban slavery in the territories. Third, it claimed that the fifth amendment of the constitution prohibits the federal government from freeing slaves brought into federal territories. The following two quotes from the decision show, not only the racial hatred, but the program of dehumanization used to defend racism against the founding documents, which claims that our rights come from our Creator and that all men are created equal. In the very same way, we dehumanize preborn children to justify the violation of their God given rights—which are protected by our documents—so that we can kill them for convenience' sake.

> The question is simply this: Can a negro, whose ancestors were imported into this country, and sold as slaves, become a member of the political community formed and brought into existence by the Constitution of the United States, and as such become entitled to all of the rights, and privileges, and immunities, guarantied [sic] by that instrument to the citizen?[114]

> We think [...] that [black people] are not included, and were not intended to be included, under the

[114] Dred Scott v. Sandford, 60 U.S. at 403.

> word "citizens" in the Constitution, and can therefore claim none of the rights and privileges which that instrument provides for and secures to citizens of the United States. On the contrary, they were at that time considered as a subordinate and inferior class of beings who had been subjugated by the dominant race, and, whether emancipated or not, yet remained subject to their authority, and had no rights or privileges but such as those who held the power and the Government might choose to grant them.[115]

Many would say that reconstruction amendments 13, 14, and 15 reversed the unjust Dred Scott decision in reality (14 in particular). A closer look reveals that the amendments were a result of a growing interposition and nullification from lesser magistrates across the country. It began when a few local and state magistrates courageously stood in defiance of illegitimate judicial overreach, weathering the storm of pressure, persecution, and personal catastrophic circumstances thrown at them by the oppressive tyrant. On each of these magisterial levels there were members of law enforcement, judges, legislators, and governors who stood in the gap against this ruling and its supporters. Even federal-level magistrates in the executive and legislative branches began treating the judicial ruling as void and without force. Lincoln's State Department began issuing passports to blacks

[115] Dred Scott v. Sandford, 60 U.S. at 404–05.

as citizens.[116] In 1862, Congress prohibited slavery in all of the current and future territories in direct defiance to the Dred Scott ruling. Slavery was abolished by the 13th amendment in 1865. Then in 1866 Congress passed the Civil Rights Act which, overriding a presidential veto, granted citizenship to blacks two years before the 14th amendment was passed. This officially reversed the unconstitutional iniquitous decree of *Dred Scott v. Sanford.*

The Fugitive Slave Act ran concurrent with Dred Scott's failed attempt to purchase his freedom and the ensuing litigation. This 1850 law required active participation from law enforcement at all levels to kidnap, detain, and return runaway slave property. It pronounced punishment on all citizens who assisted in their escape and or even failed to participate in their capture and return. The citizens had become forced conscripts to the slave catching industry. The

---

[116] President James Buchannan, who was the Secretary of State in 1847, said that free blacks are not issued passports "in the ordinary form, recognizing them as citizens, but a certificate suited to the nature of the case." *The works of James Buchanan: Comprising his Speeches, State Papers, and Private Correspondence. Vol VII 1846-1848*, page 236. Collected and edited by John Bassett Moore. Official Letter to Mr. Davis on March 8 1847 from James Buchanan Department of State. Then in 1849 John Clayton the Secretary of State said that passports "are not granted by this department to persons of color." The thirteenth annual report of the American and Foreign Anti-Slavery Society presented at NY, May 11 1853 with the address and resolutions. Published by the AM. & For. Anti-Slavery Society, Lewis Bates, 48 Berkman St. New York. 1853. Page 128. Official letter June 9 1849 from John Clayton Department of State. In 1858, coinciding with the Dred Scot decision, Secretary Lewis Cass said, "being a certificate of citizenship, has never since the foundation of the government been granted to persons of color." New York Daily Times April 12, 1858

dehumanization programs, labeling slaves as property and not citizens, were explicit denials of due process. The federal government compromised and imposed these sanctions on all of the states and territories, both slave-holding and free. This exposed the inaction and apathy of many for what it was, action towards the oppression of image bearing creatures of God.

Let's consider some of the ways local and state lesser magistrates interposed, nullifying these unjust laws and court rulings. The State of Vermont quickly passed the Habeas Corpus Law which required Vermont law enforcement and judiciary to assist and provide a form of due process to those accused of being fugitive slaves. This ran in direct opposition to the unjust federal fugitive slave act, rendering it unenforceable.

Jury nullification became a regular practice in free states. When white Americans (citizens afforded due process) were brought to trial for refusing to assist in the kidnaping and return of accused fugitive slaves, or for assisting fugitive slaves hide and escape, juries began to acquit them of breaking what was an unjust law. This nullified the effectiveness of the Fugitive Slave Act and its forced conscription of private citizens.

The story of Joshua Glover illustrates multilayers of lesser magistrates resisting the tyranny of unjust laws and rulings in coordinated efforts together. I hesitate to call this the story of Joshua Glover because it is not about the interposition of just one man; rather, the event became a catalyst to a much broader and interconnected use of the doctrine of the lesser magistrate which went on for years.

Joshua Glover was a slave who fled to the free state of Wisconsin in 1852, seeking asylum in Racine. He was able to work at a local mill in this abolitionist town which acted as a way station along the underground railroad. In 1854 his previous slave owner, B.S. Garland, found him and employed the Fugitive Slave Act to have him kidnapped and returned to Missouri. Garland and two federal marshals executed the fugitive slave act writ by capturing Joshua Glover and taking him to the Milwaukee county jail to await further transport. The sheriff of Racine (a local lesser magistrate) along with over 100 men went to Milwaukee to demand justice for Glover. Among them was Sherman Booth, a leading abolitionist and editor of The Free Democrat. He admittedly rode up and down the streets crying, "All freemen who are opposed to being made slaves or slave catchers turn out to a meeting in the courthouse square at two o'clock."[117] Remember that the *Fugitive Slave Act* required citizens to participate in the return of the accused runaway slave with threat of fine and imprisonment.

The crowd at the courthouse grew to over 5000 men as they deliberated their demands, which were quite simple. They sought a writ of habeas corpus and trial by jury for Joshua Glover. A local judge, a lesser magistrate within his jurisdiction, issued the writ. Flexing their power, the federal marshals refused to comply. This led to 5000+ men overrunning the Milwaukee Jail and freeing Joshua Glover

---

[117] Proceedings of the Illinois State Bar Association 29th Annual Meeting Chicago may 25-26 1905, Part 2 address by John Winslow (Springfield: Illinois state publishing house), 49.

themselves, sending him to Canada on the underground railroad. As an act of resistance against federal tyranny, the sheriff of Racine arrested the federal marshals and Mr. Garland for the assault that took place in the kidnapping of Glover.

While Joshua Glover made it to Canada relatively quickly, the litigation that followed this incident went on for years. Booth and a couple others were arrested; their cases made their way to the Wisconsin Supreme Court. The State court ruled the 1850 *Fugitive Slave Act* to be unconstitutional, null and void. This lesser magistrate court stood against the unjust laws and overreach of the federal government's legislators, judges, and law enforcement. The Supreme Court of the United States reversed the state courts ruling, and fined and imprisoned Booth.

The Wisconsin state legislator and the governor stood with the court in its resistance of the federal overreach of authority. In 1857 the state enacted a law to prevent the kidnapping of fugitive slaves seeking asylum in Wisconsin. There was more interposition from lesser magistrates on multiple levels in this case, but this will suffice for now.

We ended this section by showing the application of the doctrine of the lesser magistrate as found in the light of nature with the *Dred Scott* decision and the *Fugitive Slave Act*. The relevance to our topic of abortion should be obvious. In both slavery and abortion, the state sanctions the immoral practice by dehumanizing the oppressed class of people. American tyrants justify their inconsistency with our founding documents by dehumanization rhetoric and programs. This is how basic God given rights come to be completely denied.

These lesser magistrates stood on justice in their resistance to the inconsistency and tyrannical rule. They are a good example for us, who live in similar situation in our own American context. By looking at our past through this example I hope to show that this is not an instant solution. It is costly. It takes resolve, commitment, and steadfastness.

We need lesser magistrates on various levels to stand up for justice regardless of the circumstance. This calls for the support of individuals who demand that they do so. The people must make it known that they stand with and support the lesser magistrate in this resistance. Legislators, judges, and law enforcement will be putting their futures, their careers, their finances, and in some cases their lives at risk. They need the support of their constituents in these tough times to encourage them. We must all count the cost and stand with our Lord in truth. Standing for truth will come with trials.

Many of the men that stood against the laws and court rulings which dehumanized black people in our country in their defiance of tyrannical overreach lost their livelihood. Some were financially ruined, some were imprisoned. But these men of conviction and purpose counted the cost. With the support of the people they represented, their resolve strengthened. The vast majority of Christians are not lesser magistrates, but there is room for all to interpose, and sometimes that appears in the form of encouragement and support for those representatives and civil magistrates willing to stand for justice. Demand that they do their duty in executing justice, and be prepared to get behind them when they do. As you do so, remember that obedience is ours but the results are God's. Rest in His care of providence.

In conclusion let me say this is not a call to take up arms, overthrowing our government by force. It is a reminder that the call for civil disobedience is a call to submission and obedience to our God. When secular Pro-Life leaders say that we must obey the evil unjust rulings of SCOTUS as we change the political makeup of the court by electing Republican Pro-Life presidents, do you hear the voice of the serpent asking, "Did God really say not to call evil good? ... Did God really pronounce woe against iniquitous decrees that pervert justice and indirectly write further oppression? ... Did God really say that He demands us to submit our obedience to the tyrant when he commands what God forbids and forbids what God commands? ... Did God really say not to be shrewd in your own sight and wise in your own eyes? ... Did God really say to be innocent as doves and apply equal weights and measures?"

Beloved in Christ, you have been given the mind of our risen Lord and are being transformed into His image. By the work of the gospel in your life, you can stand with Him on His word and say as He did, "Thus says the Lord." The secular Pro-Life position is not the Christian position when it comes to the long-term strategy of accepting the court ruling until we can change it. We do not need a new court to overturn this injustice. We simply need to side with justice in our civil disobedience and interposition. At all costs, no matter the circumstance, we are commanded to say with confidence, "Thus says the Lord."

As Christians, we must continually be conforming to the word of God. Any deviation in our application of its teaching is sin, and we must repent. As priests in the kingdom of God we are required to consistently apply a Christian ethic, the word of God, to all our dealings in this world. This includes how we submit to and, if necessary, defy the civil authority that God in His providence has appointed. We must call evil out for the evil it is; we must never call it good. May God grant us repentance and conform us more to the image of His Son and the truth of His word. We must lay down this sinful secular Pro-Life doctrine that teaches us to trust in failed tactics rather than the sovereign working of God in providence. We must remain innocent as doves in our fight against this injustice.

PEOPLE OF PROVIDENCE: A DIFFERENT METRIC FOR SUCCESS

When it comes to how the individual Christian is to approach the topic of the government sanctioned and regulated unjust killing of preborn children, the strong current of providence should be noted as a driving force of the Christian position over and against the secular Pro-Life position. Providence cuts us to the quick as we discern the difference in primary objective, as well as the motivation and methodology to those ends. How we gauge success in this matter is defined by our view of providence. Our comfort, strength, hope, and optimism are developed out of trusting in the God of providence. This short chapter is dedicated to revealing the undergirding of the Christian position, an undergirding that is completely lacking in the secular Pro-Life position.

The secular Pro-Life establishment positions are primarily rooted in a utilitarian approach to carnal objectives and results gained by carnal means and methodology through carnal worldly wisdom of moral relativism. Their pragmatism stimulates their entire ideology and practice. The underlying principle at play is: "Do what you can to save as many babies as possible given the current conditions." And the ends justify the unjust means used to achieve them. The primary goal in the secular Pro-Life scheme is the carnal or physical result of saving babies. It is to that end that their pragmatic methodology develops. The secular Pro-Life establishment, being of the world, adopts and perpetuates the worldly wisdom that holds their position together. To them success is measured solely by the carnal result of saving babies from the slaughter. The obvious irony is the actual effectiveness and coherency in their doctrinal methods, as shown in the previous chapters.

Before continuing, let me first say that we want to save as many babies as we can. Carnal or physical results are not evil in themselves, and pragmatic methods of achieving those desired carnal results are not necessarily evil either.[118] I am very grateful to God when even one child is spared through these evil and sinful laws produced by the secular Pro-Life establishment. It is a godly desire to seek the saving of babies and the enacting of just laws. But for the Christian our *primary* objective is obedience. Our success is measured, not in the carnal results (in this case numbers of babies saved from being killed by their parents), but in whether or not we were obedient. Even as we are wise as serpents, we must remain innocent as doves. It is the compromise of truth and God's word in their worldly pragmatism that is the issue. It is the fighting of injustice with more injustice that we are against.

---

[118] For instance, applying the doctrine of the lesser magistrate is a pragmatic method to achieve a carnal result of criminalizing the killing of our preborn children.

It is not incremental steps that we are against, it is the use of unjust incremental steps that stand in opposition to the word of God that we are against. We must remember that God commands obedience, regardless of circumstance and regardless of outcome. Obedience is ours and the results belong to God.

PROVIDENCE AND THE INDIVIDUAL CHRISTIAN

The Christian is comforted by our God of providence. Christians are reminded throughout the text of Scripture that the providential care is not only to the glory of God but for the good of His children. All the events in the life of a Christian are specifically and personally designed for him as the means by which he is transformed into the image of the Son, and therefore, must be considered good.

This is not to say that the Christian does not experience pain, sorrow, loss, sadness, struggle, and trial. We are not emotionless stoics. Nor are we liars, denying the impact of sin in this world, as though pain through hardship does not exist. Death, pain, suffering, and mourning are not illusory. The sin of our first father has impacted the very fabric of all of creation as God curse it in Genesis 3. The earth still groans for the coming of our Lord to judge and complete the restoration process. Being moved from a state of wrath to a state of grace does not make the Christian immune to the temporal and physical curses in this fallen world awaiting renewal. It would be a lie for the Christian to believe and act as if he is above all pain and suffering. But we do not mourn as the unbeliever.

Our confidence is manifold. Our God is with us. He is controlling these events in our lives with care and purpose, transforming us into the image of the Son and preparing us for that beatific vision of eternal life unobstructed by sin. We are able to rejoice in our suffering as our idols, one by one, are ripped from our clutched fists and burned away in His refining fire. Christians are afforded an optimism in the here and now that the world does not know. This optimism is born out of our faith in the God of providence and enables us to stand on the Rock in obedience to His word, *regardless of circumstance or outcome*. The storm of life will hit, and we are warned not to build on the shifting and sinking sand of the world.

Our trust in God, who directs and governs all creation, dissolves the obstacles in front of us, even those that seek to distract us from our obedience. We are able to set aside the wisdom of the world for what God has said. We can do what God has said in the way that He has said it, regardless of what the world says will and won't work. We are able to measure our success by our obedience instead of by the carnal results the world demands.

As mentioned in the last chapter, our interposition on behalf of the preborn may cost us considerably. It could ruin our jobs. It could tarnish our reputation among men. We could be imprisoned or have our finances destroyed. It may cost us our lives to stand in steadfast obedience. Our confidence, comfort, and strength do not reside in any of these temporal things, but in the God that provides us all things as good blessings. King Nebuchadnezzar asked the three Jewish young men who defied him in obedience to God,

"And who is the god who will deliver you out of my hands?" Beloved, we should find comfort in their response. "O Nebuchadnezzar, we have no need to answer you in this matter. If this be so, our God, whom we serve is able to deliver us from the burning fiery furnace, and he will deliver us out of your hand, O king. But if not, be it known to you, O king, that we will not serve your gods or worship the golden image that you have set up."

As we stand for equal justice against the tyrannical state that deprives preborn children of life, let us be reminded that God may very well place us, so to speak, in that furnace. As the God of providence, He is able to deliver us, were it even a literal furnace. But if, by His infinite wisdom, He decides to leave us in the fire, we will find solace, comfort, and strength in knowing that His purpose is for our good and His glory.

This encouragement is for Christian legislators writing just laws which demand equal justice for our preborn children. They are doing this in the face of opposition from a world that hates God and loves death. It is for judges who adjudicate with righteousness and defy the unjust rulings of the past. It is for executives who lead in righteousness and set the example for justice. It is for the Christian citizen who supports these magistrates in their duty. The struggle is definite, and the trials will come. But God has placed us here for a time such as this. He has made our faces like flint and holds us resolute and unwavering in the refuge of the palm of His mighty hand.

One prophet was carried up in a whirlwind, another was sawed into pieces, and still another was thrown into a pit. An obedient child of God was delivered from the lion's mouth when he defied the unjust ruling of the king, and countless others were torn to shreds by wild beasts for their submission to God in resistance to unlawful despotism. Some chains fell away and prison doors opened, while other shackles tightened upon the imprisoned Christian. Will you, heirs of God, stand on His word, innocent as doves, and seek for equal justice, regardless of the outcome or circumstance? Christian, is this how you measure success?

PROVIDENCE AND THE NATION

In chapter 3 we spent a bit of time talking about God's work of providence. Job saw God's providence in making nations great, then destroying them, enlarging nations, then leading them away. These kings that God raises up as His servants are to lead and judge in righteousness because they are created in God's image. They are to bear the sword of justice with precision as His avenger of blood. They are to carry out God's wrath on the evil doer in proportion to the crime committed. Laws are created and enforced to that end. When they, as magistrates appointed by God, fail at their responsibility to be the axe in the hand of God, judgment accrues to their account. In all of this, God is governing His creation and directing it to its telos, preserving His creation and all that is in it. His providence extends from the ends, to the means. The hearts of these ministers of justice are like water turning in the hands of the Almighty.

The God that holds you steadfast in the palm of His all-powerful hand is the God of providence. By His infinite wisdom, He holds the flow of history in His hand, turning the hearts of kings and the actions of men into the true trajectory of all things, the coronated King's consummation. The actions (or movements) of creatures produce real effects, moving history forward. These actions of man are directed and governed by God's immutable, perfect plan and foreknowledge. The God of providence uses secondary causes, which He establishes. He upholds their essence by the power of His word. These secondary causes act and move according to their own nature. They effect the circumstances of history concurring with the decretive will of God. The Apostle Paul tells us that in Him we live, move, and have our being. The mind of man plans his way, but the Lord directs his steps. God works in and through the work of His creation. He is not dependent on creation, nor does He overpower/override the will and action of His creation for His plan. He is at work *in* their work.

Acts chapter two says that our Lord was crucified and killed at the hands of lawless men, and that He was delivered up according to the definite plan and foreknowledge of God. Acts chapter four says that both Herod and Pontius Pilate, along with the Gentiles and the people of Israel, did what the hand of God and His perfect plan predestined to take place.

Another clear example of this is in the life of Joseph, as recorded in the book of Genesis. When Joseph revealed himself to his brothers, he said, "I am your brother, Joseph, whom you sold into Egypt. And now do not be distressed or angry with yourselves because you sold me here, for God sent me before you to preserve life... So, it was not you who sent me here, but God." Genesis 50 returns to the conversation with his brothers. Joseph reminds them that they did those actions and intended evil in them, but that God intended or purposed those same actions to occur for good.

We have talked in chapter three about God's appointed servant, the avenger that is to carry out His wrath on the evil doer, who is to bear His sword of justice. He is the axe in the hand of the Almighty, says Isaiah. In His providence the king is the instrument used by the hand of God. God wields him as He wishes to accomplish His preserving work.

All this is to show that the God of providence, our Creator, is intimately involved with His creation. He is upholding it by the power of His word and directing the circumstances of history to its purposed end. He uses ordinary means, among them the actions of men, to control the movement of history, as it heads towards that final consummation and restoration.

Knowing this, we trust in the God of providence and strive to obey regardless of any circumstance. Therefore, we can say with confidence that obedience is ours and the results belong to Him. We stand on God's word, calling His servant of justice to repent and stop bearing the sword in vain. He must do his duty. The God of providence will use us to His intended purpose in this.

As we seek equal justice, in the way that He has told us to, we rejoice in any outcome God provides. We pray for God to grant our nation repentance in our dehumanizing of His image bearers. We pray for God to grant our nation repentance for killing millions of our children on the altar of selfish convenience. This He is able to do. But if He, in His infinite wisdom and plan, decides not to grant repentance to America, we praise His holy name.

It is quite possible that God will not use us as a means to bring about repentance from our national sin of partiality in the killing of millions of children. Our calls of repentance to the state may be an indictment against our God-hating nation that is being judged by the hand of the Lord. He may see fit that the accumulated sins of our nation must now be paid as the land vomits us up. Hundreds of years of denying equal justice now demand their recompense. Just as the blood of Abel cried out from the ground, the blood of our slaveholding past combined with the blood of 61 million children is crying out to God for justice. God may be handing us over to our bloodlust as a form of terrifying judgment. This may be the pit we devised, the snare that entraps us, the means of our own destruction.

HAND, FOOT, EYE: THE BODY OF CHRIST

My goal in this work has been to provide exhortation and encouragement to the professing Christian in resisting the tempting influence of the secular Pro-Life establishment. I have sought to take an honest look at the secular Pro-Life doctrine, from their own words, and to test it against the text of Scripture and the light of nature. I have done this to expose its unchristian foundation and methodology as well as its lack of effectiveness, even according to secular standards. This remonstrance was designed to walk a professing Christian through secular Pro-Life doctrine, pointing out where it sounds more like the accusation of that ancient serpent, "Did God really say?" It was also designed to encourage the Christian to stand in obedience with our Lord, united to Him and possessing His mind, and vindicate Him by saying, "Thus says the Lord." Throughout this book, I have laid out the basis for biblical doctrine in opposition to that of the secular Pro-Life. May this book be a jumping off point for Christians to prayerfully study the Scriptures, having their minds renewed and conformed to His word, which sufficiently governs and directs all our faith and practice. I believe my goal has been reached. However, I felt compelled to add two short chapters to discuss some of the implications of the doctrine we discussed and provide a few basic applications of it.

Let me begin by stating that none of the good works which I will spur you onto in love are in any way meritorious to salvation. Our reconciliation with God comes by faith alone in the finished work of Christ our Mediator. The only means to be justified before our holy God is the life unto death of our risen Lord. He represented all of His children in living a perfectly righteous life of obedience, which He freely clothes them in. That obedience led Him to a cross where He took on the sins of all those that would come to Him, and it pleased the Father to crush Him in our place, to pour out the full measure of wrath we deserved on the innocent God-Man, who drank the cup of wrath dry. It is His work alone that merits the Kingdom of God. You and I add nothing. None of our work is able to move us from a state of wrath to a state of grace. In like manner, there is no work that we can do to keep ourselves in a state of grace. That too is completely produced by Him, leaving no room for us to boast. Our justification and sanctification are about God changing our hearts and minds, conforming us into the image of the Son. Actions flow from faith, as fruit of God's work in changing and restoring our corrupted image. Our salvation, from start to finish, is solely attributed to the Person and work of Christ.

We are about to discuss what kind of life is consistent with Christian holy living, in conformity to the word of God. These works do not make one a Christian. Christ does. A lack of these works does not necessarily mean one is not a Christian. However, the Christian who is not engaged in these works is living inconsistently with the word of God. This

Christian must repent. Do not forget that the life of the Christian is one of continual repentance. As God continues to conform us into the image of the Son, the actions of our lives will be physical expressions of that change. The victory has been won and we have been given resurrection power; therefore, we strive. He died so that all those who live might no longer live for themselves, but for Him, who for their sakes died and rose again. The law said *do this and live*. The gospel says *live, and do this.*

The priesthood of all believers is a foundational doctrine to this discussion. We possess the mind of Christ. We are being conformed to His image by the renewing of our minds through the power of the Holy Spirit. We are being brought into conformity to the word of God. United to Christ, we can say, "Thus says the Lord." Obedience is demanded by God, but only the believer can walk in gospel obedience in this fallen world. We are to confront sin and corruption with the gospel and its fruit, which is our obedience by faith.

All that to say, it is the duty of all Christians to engage in this issue of injustice, and to do so in a manner consistent with our only certain and sufficient rule of faith and practice. As priests left here in this fallen world, we are to properly image God. Faithfulness to that charge involves actively standing on His word against sin, rather than living in peaceful coexistence with the culture that loves death. Our actions of Christian living (imaging God) remind the God-hating culture of the image that they are created in. It is an indictment against their rebellion and a call to repentance. So, the question becomes, "What does Christianity look like in a culture that demands the murder of its preborn image bearers?" Let us remember that every call to repentance we make obligates us to walk with the responding hearer and to bear their burdens as they respond. Repentance starts with the household of God.

All Christians, consistent in living as priests with the mind of Christ, are actively to oppose the unjust killing of our preborn children and demand God's servant of justice to stop bearing his sword in vain. This obedience, however, looks different in each Christian. By God's providential care, He has gifted each of us differently. Our resources, skill sets, talents, careers, and time are all from God and designed to be used for His glory as we image Him. Our works are as various as we are.

Your first thought of opposing abortion is probably of people standing at abortion clinics where babies are being killed. This is a very myopic view and it seems to plague the overwhelming majority of people. There must be a Christian presence at the final line, interposing on behalf of the children being led to the slaughter by their parents. But it is easy to become abortion clinic focused at the expense of all the other ways that we might serve our King in opposing this sin. The goal of this chapter is to broaden our view and present a variety of ways that Christians are able to use the resources God has entrusted them with in our fight against this culture of death.

I am grateful for brothers and sisters in Christ who are faithful to stand in the gap with me at these death camps and plead with the parents with compassion. I am encouraged by their commitment to boldly share the gospel of Jesus Christ, the message of reconciliation and forgiveness. Their call to repentance is often coupled with an offer of tangible material assistance and support. But it is not the duty of every Christian do this, although we believe that many more should participate. What does it say to our God-hating culture that loves death and demands the sacrifice of our children when there are more professing Christians inside killing their children than outside seeking to rescue them from death?

This same message of Jesus Christ, repentance, and forgiveness of sin can be brought to the public square. Direct engagement with the God-hating culture and its bloodlust *before its members go to these death camps* is a great way to involve yourself. This can be done in large crowds or through one on one conversation. In addition to shining the light of Christ to expose sin out of darkness, there is opportunity to educate from both Scripture and the light of nature.

College campuses, schools, parks, festivals, open air markets, and public events are good locations and occasions. But our evangelism and education need not be so contrived. Our God is the God of providence, and He goes out before us making preparation. God has placed us on a bus or plane next to someone; He has put us in a cab or sent us out to lunch/dinner with a coworker/friend; He has brought your neighbor over to BBQ. God has designed your life in such a way as to fill it with divine appointments of organic conversations. Let us pray for these conversations and for the courage to image Him by shining the light of Christ on the darkness of sin in truth and love. It would be helpful to view evangelism, discipleship, and education less as organized events and more as the tenor of our lives. I am always shocked in my conversations with professing Christians who are trained by the world so well that they say, "I am against abortion, but I don't think it is right to impose my morals on anyone else."

Bring the gospel into conflict with sin continually as you move about your day, wherever God has placed you. This is, in part, what it means to be a priest in God's kingdom. We apply the mind of Christ through His word that is to us the only, certain, and sufficient rule of faith and practice. Again, we ask, what does the life of a Christian priest in God's kingdom look like as he lives and navigates a culture that hates God and demands the sacrifice of preborn children?

As we think of these arenas of opportunity, let us not neglect our primary mission field and sphere of influence: the home. With the blessings of family given to us by God, it is our responsibility to inculcate them with the word of God. Evangelism, education, discipleship, and gospel living start here. Show the culture of death what a culture of life looks like. It is the duty of every Christian with a family to train them up in the admonition of the Lord, and what a glorious privilege this is. We abdicate so much of this responsibility to the secular state that trains our children with an ungodly worldview. We are also guilty of laying much of our children's biblical instruction at the feet of Sunday School teachers and children's ministry leaders. Let us resolve to take a more active role in catechizing, evangelizing, discipling our children and living it out a life of gospel repentance in their presence.

We've seen the Pew and Barna polls of professing Christians and the legalization of abortion in the introduction. In the 2018 State of Theology poll from Ligonier, only 58% of white evangelicals and 34% of black protestants strongly agreed that abortion is a sin. The broader community of professing Christians is an open market for education in a biblical world view. I have been blessed with opportunities to preach at several local congregations, teach classes, speak at conferences, and set up information booths at regional association meetings and Christian events. There are countless ways that Christians can engage other brothers and sisters in Christ, either in groups or individually, reasoning from Scripture and the light of nature and educating them on the biblical position of abortion.

Be a good citizen, in submission to the Lord that commands this of you. By applying a Christian ethic to your duty as countrymen, you are a great benefit to them, which benefits the children of God and glorifies our Savior. You will be a light unto the nations as you elucidate from Scripture what they only know distortedly from general revelation.[119] Again, ask yourself, "How do I image the living God appropriately as a citizen of this country?" I want to point out a few ways in particular that are germane to this topic.

Get involved with your local lesser magistrates. Go speak at your city council meeting (it's open to the public). There are valuable resources and videos on line showing men and women doing this very thing. Learn from them and make a habit of being a Christian voice to a dark culture.

Contact your local and state legislators. Meet with them and give them your support. Inform them of their duty to establish equal justice. Let them know you will not tolerate compromise. Point them to resources that will help them to

---

[119] This is itself a broad umbrella topic.

stand for justice. Tell them how to represent you, and how you will stand with them in the storm. Provide them with the assistance they need to resist the temptation to compromise.

If you are a lesser magistrate, I would urge you to apply the mind of Christ given to you, as a priest in His kingdom, to your responsibilities as a civil magistrate. Your Christian ethic outlined in Scripture ought to direct you in your judicial responsibilities. Image God as His servant and do not bear His judicial sword in vain. As God's appointed servant, fulfil your duty to Him, carrying out His wrath on the evil doer with equal scales. Apply justice and Stand against that which is unjust. Do not call evil good, but call it out for the evil that it is. I exhort you to fight evil with good rather than with more evil. Stand firm. Resist the temptation to compromise in your duty unto the Lord.

Think back on what was said in chapter 4 about the unjust *Dread Scott* SCOTUS decision and the unconstitutional *Fugitive Slave Act*. There were a few godly men who were faithful and stood against the beast with courage as lesser magistrates. However, the majority that spoke against the evil of slavery hid behind the court ruling in their lack of action. These cowards spoke out of both sides of their mouths, claiming to oppose evil but hamstrung and impotent to act. Weak and compromised legislators called the SCOTUS ruling unjust and unconstitutional, then they turned right around and said we are bound by it as the law of the land. We saw the same thing played out with law enforcement and the fugitive slave act, cowards who found space to disagree with the law while *just following orders.* As lesser magistrates today you find yourself in the same position. I would like to encourage you to stand firm on the word of God with courage and act consistently with what you say. Resist the temptation to compromise in your work unto the Lord. Do not walk in the footsteps of history's failure but stand with the courageous few. Our country would greatly benefit by Christians lesser magistrates applying equal justice and a Christian ethic.

The providence of God has placed each of us where we are in life. Our vocations, hobbies, platforms, and influence is from Him. Which of these resources do you have that you did not receive? They are to be received with thanksgiving and joy, to bless our lives and be of benefit to others. In what ways can we leverage them to expose the sin of child sacrifice and the injustice afforded these children under the current law?

Some will write blogs, books, and other types of literature. Some will create media such movies, documentaries, short videos, and vlogs. Some will design art work or run websites. Some will disseminate the propaganda and spread the educational information. Some will organize instructional events and activities to the death camps and civil magistrates. Some will be responsible for various media campaigns. Some will organize fund raisers for these various projects.

This is just a very small sample of ideas. The point is, there is room for everyone to use the skill sets and resources given to them by God in this fight for justice. We are not all the same and what we do will not always look the same. Let's not look down at what the foot or eye is doing, but rather encourage and support them to excel in what it is that they have to offer. I cannot tell you exactly how to fight this sin, but I can tell you that you must fight it. "To do justice means we must treat people lawfully, impartiality, proportionately, and equitably. And where we see these principles being violated, brothers and sisters, we must stand up; we must call foul; we must speak out. and when Christians call for justice, they must make sure that what they calling for meets this criteria for biblical justice."

THE CHURCH

Up to this point we have focused on the individual Christian. In this chapter we will look at some of the responsibilities of the church as it relates to the topic at hand. This aspect of the conversation can be difficult because of how the church, its function, its purpose, and its relationship to the culture at large are defined, and what hermeneutic is used to arrive at these definitions. Another difficulty is the inconsistent application of these methods and equivocation on the terms used. To avoid some of this confusion, I will start upon universal, common ground of Christian orthodoxy and branch out from there.

The mission of the church of Jesus Christ is to expand, being built up to the maturity of the mind of Christ. This is accomplished by the power of the Holy Spirit, through the gospel message preached. Jesus Himself is sanctifying His bride through his pastors by cleansing her through the washing of the water with the word. The pastor is to instruct the congregation on what God has said, to teach the local body to obey all that Christ has commanded, and to provide the individual church members with a biblical worldview. The pastor prepares Christians in his charge, as priests in the Kingdom of God, to go out and engage culture with a biblical worldview. The congregation itself acts as a built-in self-correcting defense against deviations in orthodoxy and orthopraxy.

The maturation of Christ's body happens simultaneously at corporate and individual levels. As Christ's bride is being prepared to be presented before our God, holy, blameless and spotless, the instruction to live, no longer for ourselves, but for Him who for our sakes died and rose again, necessarily impacts the individual Christian. It is by this process that they learn what it means to walk in newness of life, as one by one their idols are purged. This is where our minds are renewed by the Spirit of God, transforming us into the image of Christ. This is also how we apply what God has spoken to us regarding all of our cultural endeavors, in the context of a world that hates God and loves death. The individual and the bride, collectively, are being refined in the all-consuming fire.

Allow me to reaffirm my position on the providence of God as it relates to His bride. From the London Baptist Confession of Faith 5.7, "As the providence of God doth in general reach to all creatures, so after a more special manner it taketh care of his church, and disposeth of all things to the good thereof." It is God who established His church, and He is the one to expand, mature, and preserve her. We will be discussing the means by which God does this, namely, the members of the congregation and the pastors who are entrusted to serve them by guarding their souls.

Church discipline is vital to this maturation process. This starts with the inculcation of God's children with biblical truth. It is God that teaches them. Christ stands in the congregation, speaking the word of God to those He calls brothers. It is the Spirit of God who illuminates the word to us, opening our eyes with spiritual discernment. Our minds are being renewed by His power. God is the efficient cause of our maturation individually and collectively as His church. In His providential care for His church, God has chosen to apply the mind of Christ and His finished work to the believer through the preached word and sacrament. We will examine the human aspect of this unfailing and unthwartable work of God.

We recognize that duty and obedience is ours and that results belong to our God and King. Let the pastors among us ask themselves about the condition of their obedience in this area. The Pew, Barna, and Ligonier polls paint a bleak picture of our obedience in the area of teaching what God has said. The intake forms at abortuaries show that around 30% of abortions are procured by regular church-attending, professing Christians. This high number points to a failure in very many of our pulpits today to accurately and adequately teach what is commanded by God to His people. These polls suggest that less than 15% of professing Christians have a biblical position on abortion. Not insignificant are sins that lead parents to kill their children: the homosexual agenda, pornography, adultery, cohabitation, etc.

We have not taught what it means to be created in the image of God, nor how to image Him properly now that we are united to Christ. We have set aside what God has said about the proper function of sexuality. We have not taught what God has demanded about justice and its equal and appropriate application. In regard to abortion, we have abdicated our duty to instruct our congregations with a biblical view. Animated by ungodly fear of the government and of offending their congregations, many pulpits have acted as if the word of God were impotent, handed over the duty to catechize her members to the secular Pro-Life establishment. The doctrine of Balaam has not merely crept into the church unaware; we have opened our doors wide and invited it in.

It should come as no surprise that professing Christians have a secular position on abortion. Abandoning our duty to teach what God has commanded, we have produced generations of professing Christians who believe that the secular Pro-Life positions are the Christian positions. Even worse is the response from professing Christians that murder their children. They have been taught to presume on God's grace, and they say things like, "I'm already forgiven, the blood of Christ has covered me, I'm under grace not law." Like their father, the devil, they quote and twist Scripture to justify their rebellion. We must repent of our delinquency and teach our congregations how to apply the mind of Christ in a culture that hates God and loves death.

The failure of the pulpit greatly impacts the church's ability to exercise her authority and responsibility purge the sin from within. In defiance of the living God that dwells among His people, the church (a kingdom of priests) is refusing to "keep and cultivate" the temple. That is to say, that they are ignoring their charge to expand its borders and defend it from all unholiness.

Expansion of the temple borders does not only happen through evangelism. We often forget a crucial aspect, *families*. Beloved, have families, get married, and have lots of babies. Be fruitful and multiply; take wives and become the fathers of sons and daughters to husbands, that they may bear sons and daughters; and Multiply, and do not decrease. Catechize them and raise them up in the fear and admonition of the Lord.

Bring those children to the word and show them, through your lives, the fruit of gospel obedience. Be faithful spouses and parents. Kill the secret sins in your life and teach your children fidelity. Show them what repentance looks like as you hold fast to the message of the gospel that changes the hearts and minds of sinners. This is another area of compromise. Christian families have adopted a model that looks more like the world than the prescriptions of God's word. As the culture of death around you crumbles and implodes, be a beacon of light, sharing the hope of Christ while exposing sin as an indictment against them. Be strengthened by God's preserving hand as the God-hating world devours itself.

When there is gross deviation in the understanding or application of the word of God in the lives of Christians, it is the duty of the church of Jesus Christ to rebuke, reprove, and correct them. The church is charged to call her members to repent, to exhort them, to instruct them, and to walk with them in repentance. The unrepentant member is to be put out and handed over to Satan for the destruction of the flesh, that he may be restored, and his spirit may be saved on the day of the Lord. The church as a whole has not fostered this attitude and mutually edifying lifestyle prescribed by God. This process matures the individual and the corporate body.

Pastors often justify their weak instruction and correction. Here is a list of common responses from pastors who were asked why they do not talk about abortion and related sins. "There are too many women in the congregation that have had abortions. I do not want to make them feel bad. I want to show them compassion. It would be too uncomfortable to talk to these women like this." This is pure cowardice and it encourages the congregation to exchange the fear of God for the fear of man. While claiming to be loving and compassionate towards post-abortive women, pastors like this are in reality showing hatred for them and the men that led them there. The pastors are paving the way for continued sin in the church. In their refusal to stand on the word of God, the pastors are denying our Lord's power to forgive sins and heal His children. In a lecture on biblical justice from January 2019, Tom Ascol said this:

> What does genuine neighbor love look like? It looks like obedience to God's commands... There is no biblical justice apart from or outside of God's commandments. There is no humble walking with God apart from or outside His commandments. So, brothers and sisters, if we are going to love God supremely and to love other people sincerely, we are going to have to be sure that we are doing so in conformity to what God has commanded... To tell a man who confesses that he is sexually attracted to other men, that such attractions are not sinful, when God in Romans 1:26 calls them dishonorable passions. That is not love. That is hate. It will cause a person to go to hell, being comforted by your words...it is treating her contrary to how God has revealed.[120]

---

[120] https://youtu.be/8yebJ7uhgsE.

The same could be said about the woman who kills her own child for convenience and the men who support and facilitate the murder of their children.

The result is a congregation that has relinquished the keys of the kingdom given to them by the risen Lord. In other words, they have laid down their priestly charge to keep and cultivate that holy temple of the living God, because they have not been taught to do so. They refuse to defend its borders from that which is unholy and purge the sin from within. The women and men that led their children to the slaughter are themselves being prevented from approaching the throne of grace by cowards who are proclaiming peace, peace when there is no peace. By ignoring the gravity of sin, the congregation is hiding them in the comfort of the darkness of their sin, keeping them from both judgment and cleansing in the light of our faithful Savior.

This problem has intensified to a larger scope, infecting congregations, associations, denominations, and their respective institutions. For example, last year in Texas, an elder in a PCA church ran for the office of state governor on a pro-choice and pro-gay marriage platform. It is shameful that there was no official repercussion from the ecclesiastical structure that is in place to protect against deviant faith and practice. Churches likewise holding and supporting the *Revoice Conference* and the normalization of the homosexual agenda went without ecclesiastical discipline. A professing Christian and Pro-Life republican committee chair of state affairs intentionally blocked an abortion criminalization bill in Texas from reaching the floor for discussion (in opposition to his duty to establish and maintain justice as a lesser magistrate). He received nothing but support and commendation from his local congregation. Two years later another professing Christian Pro-Life republican committee chair on judiciary and civil jurisprudence blocked the bill, again with the support and cheers his church. These examples can be multiplied.

By stepping off the potency of the word of God, we have empowered sinful faith and practice. We have emboldened the sinner with our lack of instruction, correction, rebuke, discipline, and restoration. Revival must come with repentance. The health of a congregation can be seen in its just and appropriate application of church discipline. Let us return to our Lord's command to do so. Let us embrace the means He outlines to mature and cleanse His bride. Let us love the church and her members by calling them to repent and then faithfully encouraging them and walking with them in it, bearing their burdens—be they abortionists, workers, women who kill their children, men who support them and participate in the murder, legislators, or other lesser magistrates who fail to apply justice. Let us strive for the kingdom of God and her purity, because He is already victorious and has given us the power that raised Him from the dead. We have His word and He has given His enemies into our hands.

It is at this point that we begin to see a greater dispersion of Christian thought and practice. Due to a variety of hermeneutic devices and how they are applied, Christians arrive at a variety of conclusions as it pertains to eschatology, the definition of the church (who are members), and the role of engagement between the church and culture. Volumes would only begin to describe and defend these various positions. For now, I am going to address these overarching and often overlapping groups in their terminology, saying that they ought to be doing *something*. Then I will give a few examples of ways to get involved.

To all of my postmill brothers out there, get your neokuyperian groove on redeeming culture. Be active trampling every unholy thing underfoot and placing it in its rightful place under the authority and rule of Christ our King. Bring the reality of the gospel of the kingdom of God ever expanding on earth as it is in heaven. My covenanter friends, be the prophetic voice to our covenant breaking Romans 13 deacon and call our nation to repent, for crown and covenant. My Christian reconstructionist friends, join in defying the godless tyrants, and bring the God-hating world to submission under Christ's rule and reign. These overlapping categories of Christians and their churches have a theological grounding that obligates and defines the churches' activity.

Let me encourage my Christian friends who proudly place the American flag behind them in worship service, who are angry with the ten commandments being taken out of courthouses, who want prayer back in schools, who are elated that the president has open prayer meetings, that have fourth of July/Memorial Day services. To you I will present some examples of actionable patriotism and good citizenship by which Christians and their churches can put feet to their ideological message.

Professing Christians hold to several definitions of *church*, such as, members united to Christ only, those who attend their services, all saints from all times and places, etc. To go along with these different views of church are the responsibilities and duties of those groupings. Discussions about the obligation of churches often produce a great deal of equivocation. People shift seamlessly from one to another. To help avoid this problem, I will not use the term *church*. Instead, I will be talking about state sanctioned and regulated 501c3 nonprofit organizations and their organizational leadership. These support and provide funds for state sanctioned and accredited/or regulated seminaries and institutions of higher learning, as well as private Christian schools for all ages. I am talking about the organizations that support and fund other common kingdom functions like family camps/youth camps/young adult camps. This is for organizations that support and fund community programs like upwards sports, fall festivals, community projects, soup kitchens, and do these common kingdom events in the name of Christ. This is for those organizations that fund disaster relief and food bank programs. This is for leaders of these nonprofit organizations that officiate state regulated weddings. When I use the terms *church* and *pastor*, think state regulated 501c3 nonprofit organization and leadership in that organization.

Some very influential pastors have analogized Christian engagement with culture as polishing the brass or rearranging the chairs on the sinking Titanic. The goal of this analogy is to focus churches primarily, if not solely, on the spiritual/eternal things of the kingdom of God over and against the physical/temporal things of this common kingdom. It creates an irreconcilable, radical distinction between the two, as if they are mutually exclusive. In my experience, I often see a disengaged form of pietism arise from this line of thought, with prayers being the only acceptable offering in this spiritual battle. Prayer is vital, but not at the expense of actionable living for Him who for your sake died and rose again. Fredrick Douglas said, "I prayed for twenty years but received no answer until I prayed with my legs." This is a danger for those who promote an "either or" distinction to live as practical Neo Platonists. It can become a denial of our obligation to godly stewardship over the temporal and physical blessings bestowed on us by God, and our duty to Him in the Noahic covenant of preservation. How we steward these physical and temporal blessings in this common kingdom *matters*. God, in His care of providence, uses our rearranging of the chairs on the ship to move history forward to its ordained end. This common kingdom is not an end unto itself but exists as a platform for the kingdom of God.

Just as we saw in the last chapter on the individual Christian, there are many ways for a church to be involved. Being united to Christ we are Abraham's offspring and the Lord said of him in Genesis 18, "For I have chosen him, so that he may command his children and his household after him to keep the way of the Lord by doing righteousness and justice." As true Israel, we are told to seek the welfare of the city, for in it we find the welfare of the children of God. The homosexual agenda, the sacrifice of our preborn children, and the denial of equal justice is a detriment to society. Not only are the immediate effects themselves devastating, but the long term always causes catastrophic societal collapse. We are rapidly approaching that point. Let us ask of our churches, "In what ways are our churches stewarding the resources God has blessed us with to that end?"

Churches could hire a local full-time missionary to the preborn. By supporting a local missionary, you enable him to go daily to the death camps to preach the message of reconciliation and offer assistance. Additional duties may include other forms of cultural engagement in the public square, bringing the gospel into conflict with the culture of death, when not at the abortuaries. Such a missionary could provide education and awareness to local churches, youth groups, and other Christian functions. They could train and equip other volunteers to join them in their evangelism. Churches can provide for the material needs of this ministry.

Stop sending financial support to secular Pro-Life organizations that are offering needed assistance and tangible material help to abortion-minded women and families. Urge your congregation to do likewise. Use that money to do the Christian charity work yourselves. Offer assistance to the women directly. Stop outsourcing acts of mercy and charity to interfaith, secular, and, more often than not, gospel-hating organizations. Not only will more of your money go to actual assistance, but it makes the work personal. These women will see the work of Christian living in action, and it will provide a local body of believers for them to integrate into, if repentance and faith is granted.

Stop supporting secular Pro-Life organizations that lobby for unjust laws and fight against laws that demand God's servant to stop bearing the sword of justice in vain. A path of political expediency for career professional legislators is in line with the long-term Pro-Life strategy. Secular Pro-Life lobbyists, claiming to speak on behalf of the legislator's constituency, offer them a path of least resistance and political capital for their next election through compromise.

Let me exhort pastors and leaders of state sanctioned nonprofit organizations to spend some time with your local/city/state civil magistrates. Take your members with you. Let these lesser magistrates know that the secular Pro-Life organizations do not represent you or your Christian ethic. Embolden them to do their duty, as God's sword-bearing deacons. Strengthen them to uphold and maintain equal justice. Give them the confidence and support they need to represent you in the face of compromise. As a show of force, gather with other Christian pastors as you make these visits to your civil magistrates. Make these pleas to them a routine, so that they see the consistency of resolve of yourselves, your membership, and coalition of local Christian churches. You are their constituents. As you call them to their duty to apply equal justice, it is vital that they know you will be standing with them through the fight. Let your support for them be like Aaron and Hur, as it were, bearing them up in their weariness. The Founders ministry posted an interview with Jared Longshore and Tom Ascol on 29 Jan 2019. Here is a motivating excerpt:

> (Jared Longshore): All of the lawmakers that establish the murder of these innocents. You should be ashamed of yourselves, You need to repent and come to Christ. Jesus Christ is a great Savior for great sinners. We want to be very clear. This is the world God has called us to live in, and to be faithful

> representatives of Him. And part of it means speaking to these authorities, that have been established by God, that are absolutely rebelling against Him.
>
> (Tom Ascol): And I want to say a word to my fellow pastors. Brothers, we cannot afford to ignore these things and let them go; not talk about them; not preach about them; not pray about them. Not call upon our churches to wake up and take note of what we are living in right now. And address these things, write your legislators, call them, go to them, make them aware of your deep displeasure, your unwillingness to tolerate this type of culture of death that is being promoted.[121]

Sadly, the rarity of this allows the Pro-Life establishment to dictate the terms of compromise, which will maintain a status quo. The direct, united voice of Christians to legislators, with a withdraw of support to these secular Pro-Life organizations, will starve out the influence they have over these politicians. It will cause the legislator to strengthen his back bone and commitment to justice, or expose the hypocrisy he is resting in.

These are but a few simple examples that would have a lasting impact. Let us take this opportunity to show a true ecumenical expression to do righteousness and justice together. Regardless of our important theological differences,

---

[121] https://founders.org/interviews/the-sword-the-trowel-episode-22/.

we are united to Christ. We share His mind, and as His universal church, are to be of that one mind, with solidarity in purpose to image Him as we do righteousness and justice. Let us steward our resources wisely for the welfare of the city, because in it we find the welfare of the children of the kingdom of God. We strive as He has directed, regardless of circumstance, because He is victorious and exerts His sovereign control over all His creation. Together we trust in the God of providence as He matures us according to the counsel of His good will and is bringing all things into subjection to Him.

Made in the USA
Monee, IL
17 December 2025

39001267R00105